OUR STORIES, OUR LIVES

A Place to Rest Your Heart

The Personal Journeys of Four Women

Edited by Donna Streufert

Publishing House
St. Louis

Unless otherwise noted, the Scripture quotations in this publication are from The Holy Bible: NEW INTERNATIONAL VERSION, © 1973, 1978, 1984 by the International Bible Society. Used by permission of Zondervan Bible Publishers.

Quotations marked KJV are from the King James or Authorized Version of the Bible.

Copyright © 1991 Concordia Publishing House
3558 S. Jefferson Avenue, St. Louis, MO 63118-3968
Manufactured in the United States of America

Library of Congress Cataloging-in-Publication Data
A place to rest your heart: the personal journeys of four women / Donna Streufert, general editor.
    p. cm. — (Our stories, our lives)
    ISBN: 0-570-04560-6
    1. Women—Religious life. 2. Christian life—Lutheran authors.
I. Streufert, Donna, 1939- . II. Series.
BV4527.P56 1991
248.8'43—dc20

1 2 3 4 5 6 7 8 9 10 MAL 00 99 98 97 96 95 94 93 92 91

CONTENTS

Preface

About this new series . . .

Sharing experiences is an important part of a woman's life. Talking, listening, laughing, and crying together—exchanging ideas, advice, and counsel—being close by, being companions and sisters and mentors to one another—all are part of the experience we women share.

Women offer encouragement to one another as we share our personal struggles, our dark valleys, and our bright horizons. Women share love with a listening ear, a warm embrace, the assurance of forgiveness, or a word of counsel. Women understand when the author of Hebrews writes, "Encourage one another daily, as long as it is called Today" (Hebrews 3:13).

This book of encouragement is written by women, for women. It relates the personal journeys of four women. Their stories reflect the true-life experiences of women in many places and in many stages of life.

Each woman's story is followed by insights and analysis written by a professional Christian counselor. She uses her expertise to help the reader recognize what is going on in the character's emotional and spiritual life and offers Christian guidance and encouragement.

Next is a section designed for personal reflection. Here is an opportunity to grow in understanding, to sort out your own thoughts about the challenges portrayed in the story, and to draw support from God's Word to face those challenges. (Because Mary Lucy's story focuses on the particularly lonely and frustrating challenge of parenting a child with special needs, we have concluded the reflection on her story with hard-to-find resources of information. This section is entitled "A Word to Mothers of Children with ADD.")

Hopefully, out of all this you will be encouraged to share your own experiences with other women.

After you read the four stories in this book, give it to a friend, a sister, a fellow traveler in the faith. Ask about her feelings. Compare reactions to the story. Use it as a means for personal growth and Christian witness. Encourage. Share. Counsel. Hug. Rejoice—together—woman to woman!

Men, too, may gain insight into women's experiences, needs, feelings, and reactions through this series!

About the personal journeys of four women . . .

In the opening story, "A Place to Rest Your Heart," author Jane Fryar profiles Stava Soldar, a professional woman dedicated to her career in the publishing world. Stava feels herself coming apart at the seams. What lies at the heart of the distraction and panic she feels? Where can she find the answer to the nagging, unnerving question that echoes repeatedly in her brain: "What do you need right now?"

Stava's struggle to answer that question and to set God-pleasing priorities offers encouragement to every woman learning to cope with the conflicting values and crushing demands that are part of modern life.

In "Less Than Perfect," author Kristl Franklin tells the story of Mary Lucy, a young mother filled with love and hope for her infant daughter. Yet lurking deep in her heart is the feeling that "something's wrong and I don't know what!" Mary Lucy's tears and frustration reach a climax when Kaley one day asks, "Mommy, am I retarded?"

Mary Lucy struggles to find the reasons behind Kaley's learning difficulties. Her discoveries about herself and about God's strength and the support He provides through others will touch your heart. Hers is a compelling story that will encourage every parent whose child has somehow slipped through the cracks of the educational system.

In "Through a Glass Darkly," author Nikki Rochester profiles a mother and daughter, Kesi and Adisa. We peek into the mind and heart of both women as they sit side by side in the city's maternity clinic. "I am totally engrossed in scrutinizing my daughter," Kesi tells us. "I had poured into her everything I believed in, everything I stood for."

In this powerful story the author writes across cultural lines, reaching deep into the human experience common to us all. How Kesi and Adisa handle the anguish, anger, guilt, and feelings of helplessness that accompany a crisis pregnancy touches a chord in all mothers and daughters who have had to face difficult choices and find God's strength to forgive one another and themselves. Kesi and Adisa's struggle offers encouragement to every mother and daughter who discover their common frailty and still can't forget they love each other.

In "From Mourning to Dancing," Martha Streufert Jander tells the story of Abby Richards, 45. Abby's world is changing! Her children are growing up; she and her husband are growing apart. Her mother is growing more dependent. And Abby feels she's growing old herself—too soon.

Abby struggles to face the changes and to break the destructive cycle developing in her marriage. As she writes in her journal, we read over her shoulder. Abby reveals her thoughts on Christmas Eve . . . her feelings about handsome Dr. Tom Randall . . . her experiences juggling demanding roles of daughter, wife, mother, and professional. "I don't seem to have any time left just to be me," Abby sighs.

How Abby resolves the conflict in her heart and in her marriage and rediscovers the Christian joy that had eluded her offers hope to every woman facing midlife with fears as well as faith.

As you share the personal journeys of these women, you may find yourself in their shoes. Or you may feel yourself growing in empathy and understanding for women who face challenges you have not yet faced. Or you may know women like those profiled here. You may have a friend who could benefit from knowing she is not alone in her *own* struggle— just as you and I are also *not* alone.

Donna Streufert, Editor

Acknowledgments

In this inspirational book you are going to meet four women whose personal journeys will touch your life. The authors of these stories are also engaged in their own unique faith journeys. Take a moment to meet them.

Jane Fryar, author of "Stava," hopes other people will be able to look at Stava and see themselves. As she wrote, Jane reports she would step back and look at some of her own struggles and feelings of being overwhelmed. Jane calls Lemay, MO, a St. Louis suburb, home. As a professional editor, she produces materials for vacation Bible school. She also writes for many devotional, inspirational, and teaching resources.

Kristl Franklin, author of "Mary Lucy," is an award-winning author of articles, short stories, and novels. In 1989 she was a winner in the O. Henry Festival Stories competition. She lives in Denver with her husband and family and serves as minister of outreach in her church, teaching and training people in evangelism. Kristl incorporates in her stories a great deal of her diverse background, having worked at 25 different occupations during a 10-year span. You may even have seen her as an extra on the "Father Dowling Mysteries" and the "New Perry Mason" TV shows. Kristl wrote "Mary Lucy," in part, to fulfill her need to share some of her feelings and experiences as she and her husband raised a special-needs child struggling with an invisible handicap.

Nikki Rochester, author of "Kesi" and godmother of six, including four adolescents, resides in Baltimore, where she works as a computer systems analyst. Nikki serves as president of her church, where she puts to use her talents to sense the needs of people (parents like Kesi who wonder "Where did I go wrong?"). Because she has been blessed with the ability to apply God's Word through writing, she prepares resources for devotional and teacher training publications and edits a black ministry newsletter that reaches many churches in the southeastern U.S. "Kesi" represents Nikki's first short story writing venture.

Martha Streufert Jander, author of "Abby," resides in St. Louis with her husband and five young-adult children. She edits primary grade Sunday school materials and articles for training teachers. Her earlier works include three Arch Books: *The Visit of the Wise Men, Philip and the Ethiopian,* and *The Tower of Babel.* Martha knows firsthand the experience of women facing the physical, emotional, and relational changes of midlife, as their children become adults and a simpler life turns complex.

Shirley Schaper, a family and marriage counselor at the Davis Psychiatric Clinic in Indianapolis, wrote the counselor sections for "Stava," "Mary Lucy," and "Abby." Shirley and her husband have one daughter.

Doris R. McElwee, a psychotherapist and marriage and family counselor who wrote the counselor section for "Kesi," resides in Arcadia, CA, with her husband. For 10 years she wrote "Can This Marriage Be Saved?" a feature series that appeared in the *Ladies' Home Journal.* Doris actively serves the Lord in her church.

Donna Streufert, general editor, teaches at Concordia University Wisconsin in Mequon. She resides with her husband in Milwaukee and has contributed to a women's quarterly and written articles for a youth ministry quarterly. She regularly writes for a home devotional booklet and develops curriculum materials for the LifeLight Bible study series. Close to Donna's heart lies a deep concern for multiethnic education and a love for children, whoever and wherever they might be.

Stava: A Place to Rest Your Heart

by Jane Fryar

Stava

Stava woke with a start. She sat straight up in bed, listening. Moonlight streamed in the window. The alarm clock blinked 4:32 ... 4:33. Frightened, Stava gasped for air like a half-drowned swimmer.

Silence. And more silence. What had awakened her? Stava listened ... 4:35. Silence. She lowered her body back against the sheets and rubbed her burning eyes. She noticed a dull ache in her temples, too, the kind of ache that came when her body demanded sleep but her mind refused it.

Stava closed her eyes. She took a deep breath. Then exhaled. Suddenly she was at the office, staring at the stack of papers on her overflowing desk. Russ had been very patient. At least so far. But Stava had seen his volcanic temper erupt before, and right now at least four project managers were screaming about Stava's deadlines—mostly unmet.

Knowing the facts, Russ couldn't hold Stava responsible for the delays. At least not for most of them. Russ had attended this summer's crisis control meetings and knew Stava had done an extraordinary job of disaster containment.

Still, there were limits. Not even Russ could turn the calendar back, and that seemed to be the only hope for the projects on Stava's desk right now. Thoughts of sleep faded as Stava organized the coming day. She needed to meet with Russ, preferably before noon. If he could keep the project managers on hold for a week, even for a few days . . .

As Stava continued to outline strategy, a question slipped into her consciousness. It grew louder and more insistent. Stava frowned. The question was simply beside the point, unrelated to her plans for the morning. The question was so foreign to Stava's usual way of thinking that it seemed to come from someplace outside herself. Surely Stava would not have asked a question like it, not during a crisis anyway.

What do you need right now? She closed her eyes and shook her head as if to clear it. The question buzzed on like a fluorescent light bulb in an empty room. It refused to be so easily dismissed.

What do you need? Then, as suddenly as the question, an answer.

A priest.

She opened her eyes. A priest? Stava had a pastor. A kind man, helpful in his own way. Why would she need a priest?

She shook her head once more. The alarm clock blinked 5:10. The radio came on. Stava hit the snooze bar twice to silence it.

As she rolled out of bed and began to smooth the sheets into place, Stava remembered the appointment she had made at Oak Street Automotive. She'd drop the car off there and walk to work. Several blocks in the fresh air might clear her head.

"I need to write Bill a note," she said to herself as she turned on the shower. "If I meet Lynne for dinner at 6:30, I'll need the car by 6:00." After 15 years of friendship, Stava knew instinctively that Lynne would arrive at the restaurant no later than 6:20. The two often joked about Lynne's compulsion for promptness.

The bathroom filled with steam as Stava ran the pulse massage over her shoulders. Moments later, she rinsed the shampoo from her hair and groped for a towel. The rack was empty. Eyes stinging, Stava dripped her way to the linen closet. She grabbed a hand towel and wiped her face, dabbing her eyes with special care.

Wrapping the towel around as much of her hair as she could encompass, she stared into the closet's dimness. Then she sighed in disgust. No bath towels left; her beach towel would have to do. Maybe she could get to the Laundromat after dinner. She tossed both towels into the laundry basket as she headed back to the bedroom to finish dressing . . .

14

At 7:40, Stava looked up from her desk as Corky bounced in, coffee mug in hand. "Here. You look like you could use this," Corky smiled. "How long have you been here anyway?"

"Oh, since 6:00 or so, I guess." Stava took the mug. Strong and steaming hot—just the way she liked it. That was one thing about Corky. She always sensed when Stava struggled with more pressure than usual. And she made life a little easier for Stava when she could, whether or not it was in her job description as Stava's assistant.

"Has Russ come in yet?" Stava asked.

"No. But soon, I expect."

"When he gets here, will you tell him I need to see him? Also, I need Dr. Heckett's phone number and his file. I'm sure we discussed more changes than he's made, a lot more changes."

"Right away." Corky left. Stava stared at the pages spread out across her desk. Her adrenaline had begun to pump as she began looking through the latest (and last, or so she had hoped) version of Dr. Heckett's manuscript. Now, 20 minutes later, her stomach churned. The words on the page in front of her swam together.

Some authors took more than their share of an editor's time. That was Dr. Heckett. Patronizing. Unpredictable. But he had name recognition and a reputation as a solid researcher. "Too bad he doesn't write in English," Stava murmured.

What do you need right now? The question formed and intruded into Stava's mind before she could stop it. She squeezed her eyes closed and pressed her palms against them.

"Are you okay?" Corky asked, handing Stava a file full of handwritten notes and copies of correspondence.

Stava reached for the file. "Sure," she said. "Just a little tired. I was awake too early this morning."

"You need to take better care of yourself . . ." Corky began.

The telephone rang, and Stava reached for it. "Saved by the bell!" she smiled. Then, in a softer voice, "I'll be okay, Cork. Really I will." She picked up the receiver. "Good morning. This is Stava Soldar. How may I help you?"

15

Russ popped his head in the door shortly after 8:30. "Morning, Stava," he said. Stava looked up.

"Hi, Russ. How was golf last night?"

"Hot," Russ replied. "It must have been at least 90 out there. We should've rented a cart. Corky said you wanna see me. That Heckett thing?"

Stava drew a deep breath. "Yes. It's not working, Russ, and I don't know what to do."

Stava seldom used words like that—*I don't know what to do.* Ever since she had joined the publishing house five years ago, she had projected a super competent image. She had poise, confidence.

Almost brash at times (though her co-workers may have said pushy), Stava combined her considerable abilities with a stubborn refusal to give in to problems. Her energy and ability to work with people had carried her through three promotions and to the edge of a fourth, at least that's what the office gossips projected. The company wasn't large, but it had a solid reputation. Stava saw her present job—senior editor—as a stepping-stone to a job with a more prestigious publisher ... assuming she could keep pushing herself hard enough. She never said that out loud, of course, but those around her would not have been surprised to learn of her ambition.

What do you need right now? The question forced its way into Stava's consciousness again. Even as it did so, Stava noticed that her early morning headache had now drawn her temples tighter still. She reached into her desk drawer and pulled out an aspirin bottle.

"Let me take a look at what Heckett has done," Russ was saying. "I'll get back to you sometime this afternoon." There was a pause.

"Stava?"

"What? Oh, all right, Russ. I ... uh ... something else was running through my mind."

"Are you okay? You seem ... I don't know ... distant or something." He glanced at the aspirin bottle in Stava's hand. "Are you sick?"

"I'm fine, Russ. Just a little tired." Russ shrugged, murmured something Stava didn't hear, and left. She popped three pills into her mouth and chased them down her throat with a swallow of lukewarm coffee, her second cup of the morning. The telephone began to ring.

A flurry of calls filled the next several hours. A graphic designer with questions. An over-eager author who had mailed his manuscript three days earlier. A copy editor asking for clarification on several points.

To keep her mind occupied between calls, Stava leafed through two newly arrived manuscripts. Corky had already read both. The first, Corky's memo noted, had too narrow a focus, too small a potential audience. Stava skimmed a few paragraphs and then moved the manuscript to the thanks-but-no-thanks pile.

She picked up the second. Where had Corky's note for this one gone? Stava checked the manila envelope rubber banded to the manuscript. Nothing. She picked up the phone and rang Corky's extension. No answer. Stava glanced at her watch. 12:15. Lunchtime.

Stava yawned. A good sign. She had read somewhere that only a relaxed person can yawn. Something about the throat muscles needing to be loose. Stava smiled to herself. Maybe she wasn't slipping out of control after all. She picked up the second manuscript and began to read, a page here, a few pages there.

The author writes clearly, Stava noted. No weasel words; he says what he means in clear, definite language.

But after a few moments, Stava determined she couldn't use the manuscript. Her department didn't work with either inspirational or self-help books. And certainly not with religious ones. For an instant Stava regretted it. With a little work, the book could probably chalk up respectable sales. The manuscript said some things worth saying. Not to mention the fact that it would be sweet relief to work with a real writer for a change.

Still, Stava kept reading. A paragraph here; a page there. Midway through the manuscript, Stava read a sentence that riveted her to attention. "At heart, it's a spiritual issue," the words read. "We project a false self to others to please them.

17

We become what *they* want us to be, because we want them to respect us. We want them to like us. In the process, we lose our real selves, the selves God created us to be. We forget God's grace. We forget that He loves us as we are. We forget His forgiveness. And we forget His promise to empower us to become the persons He intends us to be."

Stava read and reread the paragraph. Then she stared at the paper, no longer seeing the words.

What do you need right now? A priest.

It's a spiritual issue. The thoughts roared through Stava's mind.

Then, silence. Near numbness. When she finally spoke, her words came out in a near whimper. "I don't want to do this anymore." Some moments later, she repeated, "I don't want to do this anymore."

Hearing herself snapped Stava back to reality. She frowned. What was happening to her? What force could churn up so much turmoil? And at such an inconvenient time? "I need a good night's sleep," she said to herself.

"I agree," said Corky, standing in front of Stava's desk. "I recommend you try to get it tonight."

Stava jumped. "You startled me. Back from lunch already?"

"It's nearly one o'clock. You didn't go, I see."

"I wasn't hungry. Besides, I didn't want to miss Russ."

"I ran into him in the hallway. He said to ask you to step into his office when you have a minute. Good luck."

Stava picked up the pages of the manuscript and stuffed them back into their manila envelope. She handed it to Corky and walked down the corridor toward Russ's office.

Whatever Stava had been expecting, this wasn't it. Five minutes into the conversation, Russ's face began to turn red. Stava felt herself becoming defensive. Her stomach knotted up; her shoulders tightened.

"I'm sorry, Russ. But the manuscript as it is right now just won't fly," Stava explained softly.

"I agree," Russ snapped back. "I agree the guy will never be named communicator of the year. But you know how these academic types are, Stava. You've worked with them before. That's why we have you. You're an editor. So edit. Work with

18

him. Get him to put his ideas into words of fewer than six syllables."

"Look, Russ. I've tried. I *have* tried. What do you think all this represents?"

Stava picked up the stack of letters and memos from the Heckett file lying open on Russ's desk. Her stomach rolled over, then rolled over again as she spoke. "I've had endless phone conversations with the man. I've put everything we've agreed on in writing and then sent it to him. Apparently he can't read. Apparently he doesn't hear me. And if he has listened, which I doubt, he's simply decided that he won't do what I've suggested. We must move this manuscript into production by September 1—that's Monday, you know—or we can forget it. It will never be available for review by May, and you can write off the possibility that any sociology department of any university will use it as a text next fall."

Russ frowned as Stava drew a deep breath and continued, "But I won't send it into production this way. It's just too convoluted. It's too confusing and too wordy."

The frown lines on Russ's forehead grew deeper. When he spoke again, he pronounced his words with a slow, distinct sarcasm. "What do you want me to do about it, Stava? I see only one option. One. Kill the manuscript. You can't do what needs to be done. You've just said that. Time has run out. So call Dr. Heckett and tell him."

"He'll say he has a contract," Stava shot back. "I wouldn't be surprised if the next time we hear from him, the call comes from his lawyer."

Russ looked at Stava—a blank look that carried a single message: end of conversation. Silence enveloped the room. Stava's knees began to give way. She had never felt this kind of physical weakness before. Tears welled up in her eyes. She blinked them back. But she found it much harder to rid herself of the anger and frustration burning in the pit of her stomach. She turned on her heel and walked out.

Stava looked busy the rest of the day. In reality, she mostly just shuffled papers. She reached for the phone to talk with Dr. Heckett three different times but never completed the call. "Tomorrow will be soon enough," she told herself.

Around 4:30, Bill called from the garage. "Your car's done, Stava. No rush. We'll be open for an hour yet."

At 5:15, Stava walked out into the sunlight. In not too many weeks, she would find herself driving home in the dark every night. Still steaming, she paced off the eight blocks to the automotive shop, wrote a check to Bill, and took her keys. She glanced in her rearview mirror and saw Bill locking up the shop as she drove off the lot.

She also saw her laundry basket sitting accusingly on the back seat. At the same time, she remembered the paperwork she had crammed into her briefcase just before she walked out of her office. Why not chip away at it while I do the wash, Stava thought.

She stopped at a Hardee's drive-up window to order a fish sandwich and strawberry shake. Within 20 minutes she sat unwrapping the sandwich as she watched her clothes tumble through the soapy water on the wash cycle.

Uninterested in her food, Stava nibbled away at it while she tried to concentrate on the pad of paper before her. She jotted notes to herself about ways she might handle the conversation with Dr. Heckett. Within minutes she found herself doodling. Words. Phrases. Job list. A caricature of Russ. Snatches of conversation from the day. She left her pad open on the table as she transferred her clothes from washer to dryer. When she came back a few moments later, Stava glanced over her doodles.

What do you need right now? Stava read. And at the bottom of the page, *A place to rest my heart.* Not quite understanding why, Stava felt her eyes brimming with tears for the second time that day.

It's a spiritual question. That's what the manuscript had said. Was it really? Was the turmoil she felt spiritual uneasiness? Sleep deprivation? Or something else? Stava decided to let herself think about her feelings, a luxury in which she seldom indulged. "Just for a few minutes," she told herself.

Soon the dryer would buzz, and Stava could fold her slips and socks and towels . . . and go home.

As she stood, still staring at her notepad, a second flood of emotion welled up inside Stava's chest. Her hands began to shake. Not that anyone else would have noticed, but the trembling was enough to frighten Stava. She took control over her breathing, forcing herself to draw in air slowly through her nose and out even more slowly through her mouth. After a few breaths, the ocean of fear that had washed over her began to ebb.

"Wow," Stava whispered. "This is scary! What is *happening to me?*"

No answer to that question came. Stava turned toward the row of dryers and wiped away a tear. Then she leaned back against one of the folding tables and watched her laundry tumble dry.

As Stava struggled through the door of her bedroom a while later, she saw the light on her answering machine blinking—one, two, three, four, five times. Five messages. A cold chill washed over her. Lynne. Dinner. 6:30.

Stava dropped the laundry basket on her bed. She sat down beside it and pressed the play button on the answering machine. The tape rewound itself, then the messages began:

"Stava, this is Lynne. I'm at the Pepper Pot. We did say 6:30, didn't we? It's 6:45. Were you delayed? I'll wait awhile." Bleep.

"Hi, Stava. Corky. I was just worried about you. I know it didn't go well with Russ today. Are you all right? Let me know if I can do anything, okay?" Bleep.

"Hello, Stava. This is Rick Jameson. I'd like to talk to you about your idea for the evangelism committee retreat. We wondered whether you could help us out with it. Give me a call when you get a chance, okay?" Bleep.

"Stava, Lynne again. It's 7:15. Where are you?" Bleep.

"Stava? Lynne. I guess you're not coming. I'll catch up with you later. Hope you're okay. Call me."

The red message light began to blink once more. Stava sat and looked at it for the better part of 10 minutes. Then she looked at her watch. 7:51. She reached for the phone and slowly punched Lynne's number.

When Lynne picked up the phone, Stava began to sob uncontrollably.

"Hello?" Lynne began. "Who *is* this?"

Stava struggled to speak. She scarcely recognized herself. Stava never lost control. Well, hardly ever. She was sometimes a sucker for schmaltzy movies. But then Lynne herself had been known to cry at the theater on occasion.

"She'll hang up," Stava panicked. But after what seemed like an hour, Lynne somehow recognized Stava's sobs at the other end of the line.

Lynne almost shouted her response into the receiver. "Stava, what happened? Are you all right? Do you want me to come over?"

More sobbing.

"Stava, you answer me right now! Do you need me to come over there?"

Silence. Lynne opened the closet and grabbed her purse. She held the receiver with her chin as she struggled into her jacket.

"Stava, I'm coming over. Unlock the door when I get there. Okay?"

Silence. Then a quiet yes.

Stava said nothing as she let Lynne into the apartment 20 minutes later. Lynne could see Stava had been crying. She reached forward to hug her friend, but Stava's body language telegraphed one word—*don't.* Lynne took a step back, then walked to the living room sofa and sat down. Stava followed numbly behind. She sat on the floor, her back against an overstuffed recliner, then picked up a pillow from the floor next to her and hugged it close to herself.

Lynne looked at Stava while Stava stared into space for several uncomfortable minutes. Finally, Stava spoke. "Thanks for coming, Lynne. I . . . I wasn't sure you would. I'm so sorry about this evening . . . I know it's no excuse, but I've had a kind of a . . . well, a kind of a hard time today."

Lynne listened while Stava explained her confrontation with Russ in a hundred words or less. In the silence that followed, Lynne looked at Stava.

"And?" Lynne prodded finally.

"And ... what? I don't know what you're asking."

"I mean 'and' as in 'and what else?' "

"Nothing else."

"Stava, sometimes you make me so mad! We've been friends forever. I've never seen you like this. One argument with Russ can't be the whole thing. You've had run-ins with him before. Be real, Stava. What is going on?"

Stava smiled a weak smile at her friend. "You know, Lynne, your listening technique sometimes leaves a lot to be desired."

Lynne smiled back. "I suppose it does. But Stava, you had me worried sick on the way over here." Her smile faded. "I admit I was angry at the restaurant when you didn't show up and especially when you didn't even call to tell me what had happened. But I'm not mad now. I'm just scared. I don't know the Stava I talked to on the telephone a few minutes ago, and I feel afraid for the Stava I do know. And love."

Stava sighed, paused, and then said, "I'm scared, too, Lynne. I ... I don't know how to explain this ... in lots of ways. I don't *want* to talk about it. I've always had my life pretty much under control. The main parts anyway. But ...." Stava chewed at a fingernail. Lynne waited. "But I don't have control right now. I work all the time and I'm not ... I mean I used to be satisfied with that. But I'm not. I'm ... Life's not supposed to be like this. At least I don't think so."

"You're spending a lot of time at the office, Stava. If you ask me, *too* much time. You're getting compulsive about it."

"I know. But it's not just the office. You understand how it is being single, Lynne. You shoulder all the responsibility— the car, the bills, cleaning the apartment, the laundry. Then I look at the women with children in our office who have even more to do, and I ...

"I get home from work, and the books I'm supposed to be reading for my night class lie there on the kitchen table staring up at me.

"Someone at the cancer society thinks I'm recruiting and coordinating the door-to-door volunteers for this neighborhood. I haven't even picked up the packet yet. And the first meeting we had to get ourselves organized was three weeks ago. Someone will call in a few days. I know they will. I don't know what I'll say.

"Tonight I have a message from the chairman of the evangelism committee at church. Last night the Sunday school superintendent called. She wants me to take a second-grade class. I don't know how or why they can expect me to do that." Stava took a tissue from her pocket and began to twist it. "I just don't know how they can expect it."

"You don't have time to do that, plus everything else you're doing?"

"No ... Yes ... I don't know. I've done it before. I even enjoyed it. But I just don't know when ... when I could do any preparation. You know, I ... I ... uh, I haven't been in church for a month, not for a meeting, not even for a worship service. I don't see how I'm going to get there to teach. Especially not every week."

"You've missed because ..." Lynne coaxed.

"Because when Sunday morning rolls around, I'm wrung out. Limp. Last week I just lay in bed looking up at the ceiling. When I finally got up, it was noon. I know that's terrible. I know it. But don't ... please just don't start lecturing me."

"It *is* terrible, Stava. But not for the reason you think."

"What do you mean?"

Lynne looked directly at Stava. "God doesn't want you hurting yourself like this. He's not mad at you for not worshiping. He's concerned about you—about you as a person, as His daughter."

Lynne paused long enough to take a deep breath, then she rushed ahead. "I know I'm not using good listening technique, Stava, but I love you enough to tell you the truth. I don't know what you think you have here. But it's not success. It's a mess. It's out of balance—your life, I mean. I love you, Stava. And I miss spending time with you. I hope that God helps you figure out how to fix it—and soon."

Stava didn't say anything for almost a full minute. A tape,

familiar by now, played and replayed itself in Stava's mind: *It's a spiritual issue.*

After Lynne left, Stava sat back down on the floor next to the recliner. She wrapped her arms around her knees and tried to think. Was her life out of balance? as out of balance as Lynne said? Stava didn't know how to answer those questions.

After chasing them around and around for awhile, Stava reached across the floor for her briefcase. She took out her folder, opened it, and tore off the page of doodles left over from the Laundromat. Snapping the briefcase closed, Stava laid it on her lap. She put the folder down on this portable desk and looked at the blank sheet of paper lying in front of her. Then she began to write.

Stava always did her best thinking with a pad of paper and a pen in hand. What elements combine to produce a balanced lifestyle? Stava printed the question in precise letters at the top of the page. Then she began to outline her answer.

Career. "Of course, that one goes down first, Stava," she said to herself in a sarcastic tone and only half in jest.

Relationships with other people. Family. Friends. Spending time with them. Helping them. Letting them encourage you. All those aspects of relationship were important.

Chores. The tasks of daily life—laundry, oil changes, housecleaning.

Fun. Stava stopped. Fun. Now there was a novel thought. She paused a moment more and then continued.

Self-care. Exercise. Shopping for clothes. Good nutrition. Long, hot baths. Without noticing it at first, Stava began to stretch her toes. A few seconds later, she laid the folder down as she stretched her neck, her shoulders, her arms, her legs. She yawned. How tired she suddenly felt. The muscles around her scalp began to relax; her headache eased slightly for the first time since morning.

"Let's see," murmured Stava, when she finally picked up her notepad once again.

"Career. Relationships. Chores. Fun. Self-care ... and ... uh ... of course—spiritual life. I knew I had left something out."

Stava glanced at her watch. 10:23. More analysis would have to wait. Stava felt herself getting fuzzy around the edges. Fatigue seemed to have shut down several switching centers in her brain. She knew from experience that she could make herself sit longer, but she could not force herself to think coherent thoughts, not after her mind and body conspired to ease her to sleep.

Late the next morning, Stava finally got through to Dr. Heckett's office. His secretary seemed surprised by Stava's call. "Dr. Heckett mailed the final manuscript the day he left town. Surely you've received it by now, Ms. Soldar."

"Yes, I have," Stava replied. "But I would like to speak with Dr. Heckett about it."

"The professor has flown to Ireland. He's presenting a paper at an international conference. He left orders not be disturbed during the trip. I suggest you call back in two weeks. He will have returned by then." Then, a click, as the line went dead in Stava's ear.

What was the word Corky had coined to describe the professor's assistant? *Efficiosnit?* Something like that. Even though Stava frowned her displeasure to Corky on hearing the jibe, Stava had to admit the nickname fit.

Russ took the news of Dr. Heckett's inaccessibility with a shrug. "If he's not available, he's not available. We've already made the decision anyway." An uneasy pause. "Right, Stava?"

"Right," Stava responded in a flat voice.

When Stava unlocked her apartment door that evening, she felt exhausted. Behind the numbness, though, she sensed a twinge of ... what? Excitement? No, nothing quite that strong. Anticipation? Yes. That was a better description.

She popped a frozen entree into the microwave and poured a glass of milk. While she waited for the timer to sound, she opened her briefcase and dug out her notepad.

The briefcase overflowed with other papers, too. Two nights ago, Stava would have considered those papers much more important than the page she had generated after her talk with Lynne.

"Time changes lots of things," Stava mused to herself, pulling the plate of sweet-and-sour chicken out of the oven and peeling back the plastic wrap to reveal the steaming food beneath it. She sat down at the kitchen table and pushed back the tablecloth. Laying her notepad next to the plastic plate, Stava picked up a fork and began to analyze her lifestyle.

Relationships. The most comfortable place to start, if indeed there was a comfortable place. Stava wrote names of the people she considered close friends. She also listed members of her family. Mom. Two brothers. Their families. Soon 12, then 14, 15 names danced on the page. Stava smiled, satisfied. Then, a question as uncomfortable as any that had ricocheted through her brain during the past week: *How many of these people have you seen or even talked to in the past two weeks? or even the past month?*

Stava looked back over her list. Lynne, of course. The two got together for lunch or dinner quite often. At least once every three weeks. "Provided I don't forget," Stava chided herself. Then there was ... her mom. Well, sort of. The two talked (or argued) on the phone once or twice a week. Funny, Stava thought. We fight most about why I don't come to see her more often.

Who else? Stava read through her list. Then she read through it again, this time more slowly. "I've been busy this month," she began to reason with herself. Excuses, reasons, explanations aside, in a few moments Stava found herself standing toe-to-toe with an uncomfortable fact: She had seen no one on her list, no one she categorized as a "close friend" in the past six weeks. Except for Lynne.

Stava moved on. Self-care. That should be a safer topic. Stava knew that she knew how to dress. Her makeup was always just right. She glanced at the notes she had jotted beneath the category the night before: Exercise; nutrition; long, hot baths.

"Strike two," Stava mumbled. She did work. And she had

walked to the auto repair shop and back yesterday. Even so, Stava had used her membership at the Y so infrequently that she had dropped it. And Corky was always on her case about skipping lunch. Stava ate too much fast food, too many microwave meals. She knew it. That truth had forced its way into Stava's awareness with clocklike regularity. Until now, though, she had seen it as a question of convenience, not as part of an overall pattern of self-care. Or lack thereof.

Long, hot baths. Stava read the words and yawned. I wish I had more time to relax, she thought.

Even as she did so, a familiar phrase floated into her mind. *It's a spiritual issue.* Stava's face flushed. "How?" Stava demanded out loud. She sat up straighter in her chair and spit her words out, rapid-fire. "I keep hearing that same line. 'It's a spiritual issue.' So tell me. What does that mean? How is any of this a 'spiritual issue'?"

Silence. Stava sighed. She picked up her pen once again, turned her notepad to a new page, and printed a precise heading at the top. Spiritual life. Then she sat back.

Stava had not necessarily wanted to tackle this topic tonight. Maybe not any night. Still, here she sat. She let her mind coast, feeling nothing, thinking nothing for several minutes.

Then it came. Wave after wave of emotion. Starting slowly, then rolling over her in rapid crescendo. Anger. Resentment. She began to write. And to cry. To write. Then to cry some more. Finally she sat back. She reached for another fresh tissue. Then she reread what she had written.

Some of it was a sheer jumble. But two clear themes appeared over and over again in an angry reprise:

Everyone—me, other people, God—expects me to be perfect.

I'm not. I can't be. I'm wearing myself out trying.

Stava blew her nose. Then she sat back to think. So that was it. It boiled down to a question of self-worth. She earned points with others and with herself by deducing their expectations and living up to them.

But there were always so many expectations, and many of them contradicted each other. Lynne wanted Stava to be available for shopping, for lunch, for long talks. Russ wanted all deadlines met, all assigned work done on time, even if that involved 70 or 80 hours a week. God wanted ... Now there was a puzzle. What *did* God want?

Stava wanted to please God. That couldn't be wrong, could it? Did He love her without strings attached, the way Lynne said He did? Maybe she'd been trying to earn His approval.

His love, too. Could that be what motivated her? Could that be what threatened at times to push her over the edge of her endurance? Was this a spiritual issue after all?

Stava found the evening's exercise cathartic. "A good cry never hurts," as Lynne often joked.

Whether the tears were responsible or not, Stava steered a more moderate course in the days that followed. She began using her lunch break to take a walk. She disciplined herself to eat nutritious meals. She took her mother to church and then out for shopping one Sunday afternoon. She even called three friends and invited them over for a Saturday evening dinner. And for once, she didn't feel compelled to dive into a cleaning frenzy before they arrived.

"I guess I've been trying harder," Stava told Lynne one afternoon on the phone. "I need balance in my life, and it's up to me to put it there. I've started to *schedule* balance, if you see what I mean. If I work it right, I can even find time to do the cancer drive thing. It's tight, but possible."

Lynne said nothing at first. Then she responded, "I'm glad you feel better, Stava. I really am. I just hope you're not doing the same old thing in a new way."

Stava felt a rush of anger rise in her chest. It took an effort to push it back down. "What do you mean, Lynne?" she asked.

"Don't be mad, Stava. I guess I'm still concerned about you, but I don't quite know how to put it into words."

Stava took a deep breath. "Don't worry, Lynne. I'm okay. More okay than I've been for a long while." Even as she spoke, though, Stava thought she heard Lynne's eyebrows rise slightly.

October came and went. The first Friday in November. 8:30. Russ stood at Stava's office door. She sat, coffee mug in hand, shuffling through a sheaf of papers.

Stava looked up. "Oh, hi, Russ. How long have you been standing there? I have the preliminary sales figures for October. Barb brought me the printout a minute ago if you're interested."

"Not really, Stava. I . . . uh . . ." His voice, much flatter than usual, trailed off.

Stava noticed the cardboard box in his hand. She straightened in her chair. "What's up, Russ?" she asked.

"I'm on my way to pack up my office. I wanted to tell you myself."

"Tell me what?" Stava frowned in confusion.

"I resigned this morning."

"But . . . but why?"

"Don't sputter, Stava."

"But why, Russ?"

"Because I didn't like the alternative."

"Which was?"

"Being fired."

"Oh, Russ!" Stava stood up and started toward the door.

"Don't, Stava. Let's just keep this short and sweet. I wanna put my stuff in this box and get outa here."

"But Russ? Why did . . ."

"They cited several examples of mismanagement. You know about this summer's problems. The department's bottom line. But mostly it was the Heckett fiasco, I think." He paused, then continued, "You don't know yet, do you? Heckett's lawyer called yesterday. They've decided to sue. I don't believe we were in the wrong. But the legal system being what it is, we'll probably wind up paying them a percentage of the amount they're asking. Breach of contract. Something like that."

"But Russ, all of that was *my* fault, not yours. I'll go tell them. I'll go see Nelson myself!"

"Don't get hysterical on me, Stava. And don't go setting yourself up to be shot down for my sake, especially not with the CEO. They'll tell you I should have run a tighter ship.

That I should have managed you more closely. You'll probably get the ax yourself, and it won't help me one whit. The company needs a sacrificial lamb. I'm it. It's that simple." His voice softened. "Besides, someone who knows the department needs to stick around to pick up the pieces. You're the logical one."

Stava felt as if her brain had gone on hold. She fumbled for words. Nothing would come out.

"One last thing, Stava. It was not your fault. Don't let yourself think that it was. It just happened. Sometimes things just happen. You do the best you can, knowing what you know at any given time. But you can't control everything. You can't defend yourself against every contingency. You watch out for the most likely ones. And sometimes you take a side hit."

Then he was gone.

Stava sat, stunned. Before she had time to decide what she felt, Corky came in. "The corporate office called," she said quietly. "Mr. Nelson wants to see you. Now."

Stava felt next to nothing, saw next to nothing as she walked down the corridor and got on the elevator that would take her to the president's office. She sat stiffly in one of the chairs in the anteroom, waiting for a summons. Questions barraged her mind. If she were to be fired, Russ would have done it. Or someone on Russ's level. At any rate, it would not be Mr. Nelson. Would it?

Stava didn't have enough time to think through that question. As soon as she began to analyze it, Mr. Nelson came out of his office to usher her in. Stava found herself in a daze as she listened to his quiet voice. He flipped through her personnel file as he explained the company's confidence in her.

Stava's thoughts leapt from one conclusion to another about his purpose until, finally, the bombshell dropped. Mr. Nelson closed Stava's file, looked up at her, and announced, "Stava, we want you to head scholarly books."

Stava felt her eyes widen. She let out an involuntary gasp. "Now, don't contradict me," said Mr. Nelson, diverting her protests. "We've seen your work, and we know you can do the job."

Stava returned to her desk an hour later, her mind a blur. She picked up the telephone and called Lynne. "Meet me for lunch?" Stava asked.

"Oh, I suppose I can squeeze you in," teased Lynne. "When?"

"Now?" asked Stava.

"Now? Stava, it's 10:30."

"I know. I need to talk."

Stava sat in the sunshine of a back booth, nursing a cup of coffee when Lynne arrived. Lynne didn't like fast food places, but at least this one had a glassed atrium and several green plants. She ordered an orange juice and walked over to Stava's table.

"Hi," said Stava, scarcely looking up.

"So what's the deal?" asked Lynne.

"Russ quit this morning. He quit so they wouldn't fire him. So they wouldn't fire him for my mistakes."

"Wait a minute. Are you sure that's accurate?"

"We're being sued. I'm the one who worked most closely with the author who's bringing the case."

"So you're taking the blame?"

"You haven't heard the whole story yet."

"What else?"

"They want me to take Russ's job."

Only the clatter from the kitchen broke the silence of the next few minutes. Stava sat, head down, and stirred her coffee.

"What do you need right now?" Lynne's question startled Stava. At first she didn't know whether the words had come from Lynne or from inside herself.

"A priest," Stava whispered.

"Excuse me?" asked Lynne.

"That question. Back in September that question kept coming to my mind. It . . . I couldn't get rid of it. At first, it was just a question. Then, after a while, it always answered itself. 'What do you need right now?' 'A priest.' It all seemed so confusing. So . . . well, ridiculous. It still does. What . . . what do you . . . I mean, do you understand it, Lynne?"

"No. At least, I don't think so. Tell me what you think when you hear the word *priest.*"

"I don't know. I've never known a priest. All I have is a sort of impression. I know it's unrealistic, maybe even juvenile, but I . . . I don't know. I guess I expect that a priest would be someone who knows me better than I know myself and who knows God really well. Someone who knows both of us in-depth and could maybe . . . well, could maybe bring the two of us together. Pretty stupid, huh?" A single tear ran down Stava's cheek. She didn't wipe it away.

Lynne looked at her friend. Then she said softly, "Stava, you've just described Jesus. Our High Priest, you know. Like the Bible says."

"But why would I . . . I don't understand what He has to do with all this."

"Tell me what you're feeling."

Stava began to stir her coffee once again. Finally she spoke. "I guess I feel lost. Like I've lost myself somehow. I don't know who I am anymore. I know what I *do*, but I don't know who I *am*. I'm so tired all the time. I should have seen the problem with Dr. Heckett coming, Lynne. I just missed the cues. Or let them go past."

She paused, then went on. "And I feel ashamed of myself. Ashamed that Russ lost his job because I'm incompetent. If I had been more on top of the situation, none of this would have happened."

"Those sound like spiritual issues to me, Stava," Lynne said softly.

Stava looked up at her. "You're going to tell me I don't have to feel guilty because God forgives me. Right?"

"Wrong. If you've sinned, He does. But that's not what I was going to say."

"Then what?"

"I hear you saying you feel like a failure. Like a failure as a person."

Stava tried, but she couldn't hold back the tears. She picked up a napkin and dabbed at her eyes in a futile effort to keep her mascara from running down her face.

"That's what bothered me when we talked a while back, Stava. Remember? You kept saying you just needed to try harder, to organize your schedule more. Then you could handle all the parts of your life. Remember?"

Stava nodded, still blotting her eyes.

"Well, Stava," Lynne said gently, *"doing* things won't make you a worthy person, no matter how many things you do. Stava, you don't have to make yourself acceptable. You've already been accepted."

Stava silently repeated Lynne's last sentence. Then she said, "I don't understand what you mean."

"Look across the street, Stava."

Stava glanced out the window. Then she looked back at Lynne with a blank stare.

"Christmas decorations, Stava. The department stores have already taken down Halloween and are putting up Christmas."

"So much for Thanksgiving!" Stava said with a bit of sarcasm.

Lynne smiled. "Christmas is the key, Stava. The key to who you are."

Stava looked at Lynne blankly. "Don't you see, Stava? God created the world with you in mind. Knowing you'd sin, knowing He'd have to send Jesus to die for you. Knowing all that, He went ahead anyway. He wanted you, Stava, but not so you could slave for Him all your life."

"Then why?" Stava interrupted.

"Because He loved you, Stava. Because He wanted to bless you forever and ever. God doesn't want your service, Stava, or your achievements—no matter how great they might be— He doesn't want any of that nearly so much as He just wants *you.*"

Lynne sat back against the back of the booth. Stava began to stir her coffee once again. At last she spoke. "I know that. At least intellectually. I am a Christian, Lynne."

"I believe you are, Stava. But knowing about God's grace in your head and letting it sink down into your heart are two different things. And walking it out in your life . . . well, none of us has fully managed that yet."

Stava sighed quietly. "So you think I shouldn't feel bad about taking Russ's job?"

"I think you have a bigger question to answer first."

"Which is?"

"What are the priorities in your life? No, I said that wrong. What are God's priorities for your life?"

As Stava unlocked her front door early that evening, she knew she would spend the next several hours with her notepad. I'm glad it's Friday night, she thought. I can take whatever time I need without thinking about getting up in the morning. She heated a can of vegetable soup and got down to business.

Priorities. Goals. What did she want to do with the rest of her life? What did God want to do with the rest of her life?

The answers to those questions would not come. The longer Stava sat, the more uneasy she became. Piece by piece, the truth began crashing down around her. A few hours before, Stava had heard Lynne tell her the truth, but it had seemed as though Lynne's words applied to someone else, someone "out there" someplace. Now the truth of those words honed in on her heart, landed with a thud, and began to explode the myths that Stava had come to believe about herself.

It hurt. At least parts of it did. Had she done everything she had ever done simply to prove her worth to others? Well, maybe not everything. And even if some of that motive had tainted her actions, did that necessarily make them all worthless? Stava remembered reading a remark by William James, the psychologist. Something about it being nearly impossible to overestimate the human craving to be appreciated. Craving. Stava couldn't be sure of the rest of the quote, but she was certain of that word.

Even so, Stava wouldn't let herself wiggle off the hook that easily. The imbalance, the chronic fatigue, the frustration and irritability she lived with on a daily basis testified that Stava's need for approval, for self-esteem based on measurable achievement, had gotten out of hand. What had Lynne said? You're a worthwhile person because of who you *are* as God's daughter rather than because of what you *do* for Him or for others.

Of course, that could never excuse self-centeredness or laziness. It could never excuse someone who ignored the needs of others around her. "But if I don't take care of myself," Stava reasoned, "before long I won't be able to care for anyone else either."

What do you need right now? The question came back to Stava with such force that for a moment she thought she had heard the words form aloud in the air around her. This time she spoke the answer to the question herself, "I need a priest."

Stava hadn't prayed for weeks, maybe months. She had gone through the motions mentally, but had not really opened her heart to heaven. This time it was different. She felt compelled to kneel, then to lie on her face before her High Priest. As she did so, the confusion, the fear, the sin came flooding out. Anger. Resentment. Bitterness. The sense of loss she felt. The frustration. All of it rushed out in a torrent.

Stava didn't notice at the time, but the wall that had stood so long between Stava and her Savior fell and was swept away in the surge of her confession.

Stava couldn't be sure how long she lay on the floor. An hour. Maybe two. It didn't matter. When she got up, she went to find her Bible. She curled up on the sofa, wrapped herself in the blue afghan her mother had made for her, turned to the Psalms, and began to read. In the comfort of forgiveness, the heavenly Father held Stava, soothed her.

A place to rest my heart. "That's what I need," Stava told herself. "That's what I've always needed." She fell asleep on the living room sofa and awoke 12 peaceful hours later, well into Saturday afternoon.

"I don't think it's wrong to have personal goals. I mean, it's not necessarily selfish. Do you think so?" Lynne asked as she cut into her baked potato at the Pepper Pot on Sunday after church. "You know, like hobbies and things."

"You're referring to your model train set, I presume?" asked Stava with a smile.

Lynne grinned back. "Sure. I know I'm a bit demented, but I really enjoy it. I've created a whole other world. An alternate reality, all in my spare bedroom. I don't really need the space for other things, and I enjoy puttering around with the trains. It helps me relax."

"I think it's okay," assured Stava.

"Well, I don't know. They *are* kind of expensive. But I knew that when I got started. I just enjoy it. Like I said—demented."

"I don't think so. I just haven't let myself take time out for anything that didn't have some larger purpose, whatever that means."

"I think it means you want your life to count for something. And that's okay."

"Yes. But I've taken it to extremes," admitted Stava.

"Even God rested on the seventh day. When was the last time you gave yourself a day off?"

Stava snickered, then looked down at her plate. "I confess." Then, looking up into Lynne's eyes, "But that's the past. By God's grace, it will change. It *will* change, you know."

The conversation now suddenly sober, Lynne asked, "Have you thought any more about what you're going to tell Mr. Nelson tomorrow?"

"That's all I have thought about most of the weekend," Stava said. "As I see it, I have three options. One—I can take Russ's position. Two—I can refuse it and ask to stay where I am. Three—I can resign and start fresh somewhere else.

"A manuscript came across my desk awhile back. We couldn't use it, because it wasn't the kind of piece we do. Kind of a . . . well, at the time I thought of it as part of the self-help genre. But now, I don't know. I think it tried to give the reader a feel for this whole issue of self-esteem and personal worth from a Gospel-centered point of view. It did a good job. I wish I had the chance to read it again."

"What are you saying, Stava? That you'd like to find a publisher that works with that sort of thing?"

"It's one thought."

Lynne nodded slowly. "Just be sure," she said. "Just be sure you don't start to think that fighting this battle will be any easier someplace else. You're still you, Stava. A new job in another place won't change that."

Stava nodded soberly.

She wore her best suit Monday morning. She stopped at the Pepper Pot for a decent breakfast before going to the office.

"Good morning," Corky said promptly at 7:40, as she handed Stava a mug of steaming coffee. Stava smiled a thank you and then turned back to the page on which she had been working. Corky stood for a moment looking at Stava, then she silenced her curiosity and left.

At 8:55, Stava got up from her desk and put on her jacket. "The longest mile," she mused to herself as she thought about the walk she was about to take to the corporate office. That's the way she had felt about it last Friday. Her stomach and her mind were calmer today.

Stava took a deep breath, looked around her office, and walked down the hall to keep her appointment with Mr. Nelson.

An Encouraging Word

What plans does God have for me? Who am I? Where are my boundaries? When should I say no? What are the limits to my time, my energy, my job? Where is my place in the career world? Can I handle all the pressures of a heavy work schedule and manage my personal life too? I can't handle this pressure anymore. Should I cut back? Where? What will people think? What if I miss this deadline? Have I failed? Will I be labeled inadequate? Would a career change or a promotion help?

Have you ever asked yourself those questions?

How much simpler life would be if, with our baptismal certificate, we received a blueprint outlining God's detailed plan for our lives with every *t* crossed and every *i* dotted. If only a voice from some passing cloud could announce, "Here is your spot in the world. This is where you will shine. This is the place you should work. These are the people who will be best as your co-workers. These are the people who will help balance your unique personality. Here is where you will feel most comfortable and be most productive. Here is where I want you to serve."

But it isn't that simple.

Stava is experiencing the frustrations of balancing her life, of setting limitations, of accepting herself as a human being. She is getting in touch with the fact that she is created, forgiven, and sanctified by God, but still human. She is caught in the struggle of setting goals too high, resulting in a continual striving for the unattainable and the somewhat undefined. Stava's feelings of confusion and frustration stand in strong contrast to the opinions others hold of her. They see her as a high achiever, who looks as if she has it all together. This is Stava.

And, this is life. People tend to regard some of their peers as strong and others as weak, when in truth each of us is a composite of strengths and weaknesses. Sometimes our strengths predominate, other times not. Yet, once others see us as a strong individual, or a weak one, they tend to freeze us in that frame, no matter what. Stava's freeze frame presents her as a tower of strength, no matter what.

In searching for sense and peace, some people turn to astrology and the stars for answers. Others may use psychics or crystals, or vainly attempt to achieve the answers in an altered state of consciousness. Stava is working through this stage of life depending on her experience. She is living it. She is figuring out what works and what doesn't. She is turning to her friend Lynne and to her God for guidance. She also talks often with herself. It is as if she is her own best friend, as if she is giving herself some very good advice. She counsels and consoles herself.

Stava is a unique and talented young woman. She struggles with her own identity. She is not yet fully aware of her uniqueness. She also is not fully aware of her talents and her strengths. She sometimes pushes herself in ways that become uncomfortable. When the pieces of life don't fall into place, she feels the pain and arranges the pieces in a different way. She seeks balance in her life. She tries to set priorities. She makes changes. She is learning from experience. She is discovering new ways to arrange her life that will give her control again.

Stava stands at a crossroads in life. She has had a job with the same company for some time now. Behind her lies one of the first big hurdles women face early in their careers when they wonder if they are good enough to do the job.

She has cleared that hurdle; she has proven herself on the job. Nonetheless, doubts linger in her mind, because in reality she has arrived at a new stage of development. A larger picture confronts her. She is a juggler trying to balance job, home relationships, and leisure activities. She becomes acutely aware that she could possibly fail at all of them.

Who is Stava? What kind of personality does she have? Why does she react the way she does? Why does she choose quiet introspection and personal conversations with her friend and with God to work through this developmental stage of adulthood?

Stava, like 25 percent of the American public, tends to be more an introvert than an extrovert. She is a friendly, sociable person who by nature gets so wrapped up in her responsibilities and her work that she forgets about reaching out to others.

An Emotional Sponge

Stava also is the type of woman who introjects or unconsciously takes the feelings and problems of others into her own personality. In a sense, she is an emotional sponge. Therefore, instead of finding support in the company of others, at times she feels even more burdened. Interacting with others sometimes saps her energy. For example, Stava is aware of her boss's problems. His difficulties make her stomach churn. She fears going to the president's office both when she is being offered the promotion and when she returns with her decision. Her mother's needs nag at her. She should have more personal contact with her mother, spend more time with her. Stava acknowledges trying too hard to be a people-pleaser. Somewhere she read that to enjoy a balanced life she needs to spend more time with friends. However, this does not always work for her. Rejuvenation in her case may need to come in another way or from a new and different kind of contact.

The beauty and value of being an introspective person is that renewal often is no farther away than an hour or so off by one's self, enjoying a solitary walk, listening to music, or quietly cocooned behind a closed door. No apologies are needed for reserving and protecting time for reflection and self talk. We can fulfill our responsibilities to others and also keep time for ourselves. Reading for some people proves to be a source of comfort and renewal. Stava chose the Psalms for meditation. What an excellent choice! Here she experiences the recognition and acceptance no human friend can provide. Here she is able to converse with her God as she can with no one else. And God listens in a way that Lynne or no one else can. Stava, the emotional sponge, will always be picking up someone else's feelings, which might interfere with her own self-expression and self-awareness. In her quiet times she turns this characteristic into an ally. She puts her sensitivity to work, taking in God's forgiveness and acceptance as she reads His Word. Time alone and apart proves to be a source of renewal for Stava.

Naturally Intuitive

Stava also seems to be naturally intuitive. More important, she has learned to heed her inner leading. She seems to know intuitively that a lawsuit would be the end result of the cancellation of Dr. Heckett's manuscript. She is aware that she is burning herself out, that she is overscheduled. Her intuition minces no words, "You've got to balance your life. Set priorities." An internal voice continues to lead her. She is intrigued by the manuscript that talks of "spiritual answers." She desires to take these spiritual answers and integrate them into the rest of her life. Stava's example teaches all of us an important lesson! Capitalize on your God-given strengths rather than emphasizing your weaknesses. Make the most of your assets.

When Your Achievements Are Your Problem

We quickly see other strengths in Stava. She meets deadlines, makes schedules happen, keeps promises. Being organized seems to come naturally for her. She gets things done. Her superiors at work have noticed, have promoted her in the past, and are offering yet another promotion. They recognize the fact that they have a "good deal" in this employee. She will probably work longer and harder than the rest of the staff. She won't complain, and she will get results. A team player who makes other people feel good, Stava is a desired person to have on board.

As we have noted, Stava's strengths at times become her primary enemy. Being an achiever and a pleaser, she faces the powerful temptation to try to top her own achievements. Unconsciously perhaps, she is in competition with herself.

Thus, her achievements may pose her biggest problem. If she can slow down and give herself some downtime and alone time, she will find that priorities will realign themselves, and the pieces in her life will fall into a more comfortable pattern.

Stava doesn't tell us whether or not she accepts the promotion offered her. It probably doesn't matter. Wherever she works, she will continue to bring along her uniqueness and her loveability. She may not always feel valued. She may not get a lot of recognition. She quietly, faithfully handles her responsibilities without fanfare or bragging. At times others may even overlook what a valuable and unique person she is. But anyone who takes time to look closely at any system in which Stava is working will recognize her value.

The Place to Rest Our Hearts

The fact that so many people and systems intrude into Stava's life and make demands on her time can be seen as an indicator of this talented young woman's value and worth. Her mother, her church, the cancer society, and her boss need what she can do. They want Stava's participation; they value Stava's contribution.

A critical question for Stava, however, is if she is able, without withholding herself, to keep clearly in focus that her worth and value are based not on what she achieves, but on who she is. God has made her a valuable person, and in Christ He offers her permanent worth. Her heartfelt cry for a priest reveals a deep yearning within all of us. We want the assurance that God accepts us, even though we haven't made the grade. When Stava's heart finds rest in that assurance, she regains energy and perspective to befriend herself and to restore balance to her life.

Choosing Models

As Stava's story ends, we see her learning balance by looking closely at her friend Lynne's life. Finding realistic role models can help each of us to get a clearer perspective on ourselves. Lynne seems the opposite of Stava in several ways. She is an extrovert. She knows how to play. With aplomb she invests time, money, and energy into her model train hobby.

She knows how to relax. Stava moves closer to a balanced life because she has a good friend like Lynne. God has made people different from each other so that we can complement each other. Part of life's challenge includes seeking out friends who are good for us, rather than harmful to us. Equally exciting, we can offer healthy friendships to others. The reader can be assured she will be a good friend for life, and those close to her will reap many benefits.

Stava truly is a piece of God's beautiful creation. His handiwork shines out through her personality. The unique balance of Stava's creativity, intelligence, intuition, organizational skills, and caring nature are well defined. When Stava finally learns to rest her heart in the value and worth God gives to her, she also gains the necessary strength to say no at appropriate times, to take care of herself, and to set limits. She will not burn out. She will glow quietly, steadily. Once in awhile someone else will notice her beauty and point it out for others to see. Stava will probably not do this herself. She is not a show-off. She will enjoy being on display for awhile. She will appreciate the fact that others notice the talents God has given her. She will slowly learn that what God has made in her is uniquely good. It is Stava, and it is beautiful.

Shirley Schaper

Reflection

- How like/unlike Stava are you? How closely does your personality match hers?

- Skim Ephesians 1. What does this chapter have to say about your identity? Why is knowing your identity as a child of God through Christ Jesus so important as you seek to live a balanced life?

- If you feel constant tension ... if you become anxious at the thought of sitting still for a few minutes in traffic ... if the thought of relaxing for a few hours on a Saturday afternoon makes you nervous ... you may want to ask yourself some serious questions about your lifestyle. Use a notepad. Keep track of everything you do for a week. At week's end, analyze your list. How balanced or out of balance is your life? Do you have time for work, for rest, for self-care, for friendships, for helping others, for spiritual growth and refreshment? Does any one of these things take up a disproportionate amount of your time?

- Have you set goals for your life? If so, think them through. Compare your goals with the way you've used your time during the past week. Ask yourself, "Will I reach my long-term goals if I live a lifetime of weeks like this one? What could/should I change to make my daily activities more congruent with my long-term goals?"

- Do you suspect any part of your life might be out of balance right now? What leads you to think that? How might confession, absolution, and yielding to God help you regain balance in that area? Who might help you with this process?

- Get advice from a close friend. Talk to your pastor. Above all, ask your heavenly Father for help in deepening your understanding of yourself as His precious, dearly loved child. The more you draw on that identity, the better able you will be to set goals and priorities for your life that bring peace to your heart and honor to your Savior.

Heavenly Father,
I belong to You.
My life and strength are Yours.
You put me together
In a special way
To fit Your special purpose.
You own me.

Heavenly Father,
I belong to You.
My weakness
My failure
My sins
You paid for—in Christ.
You bought me back.

Heavenly Father,
I belong to You.
Make me wise.
Help me spend myself
In ways
That please You.

Amen.

Mary Lucy: Less Than Perfect

by Kristl Franklin

Mary Lucy

Her eyes are closed, face turned toward us, when Dave and I first see her. We tiptoe to the crib and look down on the tiny, sleeping baby. She's small for an almost four-month-old infant, but her cheeks are plump and her fists are chubby. Her mouth looks like a miniature, pink rosebud, reminding me of the teacup roses my grandmother once grew near her front porch.

Dave gently traces his finger over one delicate ear, and, at his touch, her blue eyes open. Encouraged, he gathers her into his large hands and lifts her against him.

"My, what a sweet little angel!" he exclaims. He's practically crowing! I've never seen him so affected in the five years we've been married. I watch in amazement as Dave cuddles the child we're adopting. His six-foot-four frame seems an unlikely backdrop for the lace-dressed child in his arms.

I'm surprised at myself, too. Somehow I imagined this moment differently. Isn't it the mother who is supposed to hold her baby first? And here I am, shyly hanging back, completely overwhelmed by the moment.

Then Dave holds out the baby to me, his eyes sparkling. His smile for me is soft with unabashed love.

"Mary Lucy," he says, making my name sound as soft as a sigh. "I would like you to meet Kaley Rose, our firstborn."

Just at that moment, her eyes meet mine. Square on, without flinching, her soft eyes stare at me. The look she gives me seems filled with calm trust, as if some deep wisdom senses the love that will bind us together. It must be my imagination, of course. Babies can't know about "love things," like commitment, determination, and hope, just from looking at someone. Can they?

Our little Kaley Rose, during the first four months of her life, was a nameless infant shuttled from hospital to foster home and back. When I first heard about her, Kaley was already known in the foster parents' network, with which I had contact, as "the baby who can't stop crying." Intrigued, I decided to find out more about this baby. I learned from her social worker at county welfare that test after test had been run to find out why this baby's only response to her world was an ear-piercing wail, but the tests showed nothing definite.

When I told Dave about her, all he said was, "They probably don't keep her feet warm enough." As the oldest in a family of six siblings, he fancies himself quite an expert on child care.

Unfortunately, a pair of booties isn't enough to solve this baby's problems. In fact, the doctors at Children's Hospital predict a bleak future for her. Based on her behavior patterns, "soft" neurological signs, and possible Minimal Brain Damage (cause unknown), they felt she was "unadoptable" and advised she be placed in institutional care.

The social worker told us, "At best, you'll be dealing with hyperactivity, behavioral problems, and learning difficulties. At worst . . . well, even the doctors don't know what the worst could be."

Dave and I had talked about adopting a child even before our years of childlessness. During recent months we have been actively seeking a child, but we hadn't found the "right" one for us.

Until now.

"Loving a child with special problems can be very hard," the social worker counseled.

"Loving anyone is very hard," I said, probably sounding more confident than I felt. "We'll deal with problems as they come."

"I just want you to understand fully the situation before you get too involved," the social worker continued. "This little kid could break your heart."

But by that time it was too late. For whatever reason, God has placed this little baby in our lives. She is our daughter. We both knew before we even saw her that she is ours.

Oh, how I want to prove the experts wrong. I want Dave's and my love to be able to change her ... to make her strong and whole. Still, as much as I try, I can't forget the doctors' predictions and the social worker's words. I tuck them in the back of my mind, hoping they won't come back to haunt us.

We bring her home to the little A-frame house Dave has built on an acre tract deep in the foothills. The first snowflakes of the year swirl around our VW, engulfing me with peace despite the wailing infant in my arms. Yes, I will prove them all wrong. Ye of little faith, I think of those who don't believe she will be all right. I will fill her days with warmth and love and security. And tears, I soon discover. Not only hers but mine as well.

From the moment we arrive home, I hold her against me, trying to cuddle her, trying to soothe her. This is more difficult than I thought, because her little body is stiff, unable to relax and mold against mine. She has a tremor along her right side, and her leg is twisted slightly inward because of a bone deformity.

At four months she is underweight and still wears newborn diapers and clothes. It's obvious she hasn't received the proper nourishment. This now comes as no surprise to me. After all, how much food can you get down a screaming infant?

She cries unceasingly. Our pediatrician tells us it's impossible for a baby to cry nonstop for longer than 20 minutes. But Kaley once cried seven hours straight without pausing to catch her breath.

That first week, starting in the mornings, I'm greeted by screams coming from her crib. If I delay too long in feeding her, she becomes inconsolable and unable to suck her bottle or so upset anything going down will come right back up.

Fortunately, when I learn her feeding pattern, her eating improves, because I have a bottle or cereal ready before she feels the first hunger pang.

She continues to cry; I continue to hold her. Soothing warm baths, gentle back rubs, and silly songs help a little.

Dave rocks her every chance he gets. So far he has broken two rocking chairs in the process. It's clear she adores her dad, and he calms her when no one else can.

At the age when other babies are cooing and laughing at the silly faces their parents make, Kaley has never smiled. Dave buzzes her bare tummy with his lips, looks up, and plays peekaboo. "Hey, Boo," he says. "I love you." Finally one day she smiles back at him through her tears. But she cannot smile or laugh without crying at the same time.

One hot summer evening, Dave comes home from a long day of checking and repairing telephone cables and finds me sitting in the middle of the living-room floor. I'm on my knees, rocking Kaley back and forth. Both of us are sobbing our hearts out.

"I don't know what else to do," I manage to say, wailing louder than the baby in my arms. "I've tried everything, and nothing seems to work! Just loving her isn't enough."

Dave doesn't even take off his helmet or tool belt. He unlocks my stiffened arms from around the baby and takes her. Then he leads me to our bed and tucks me in. I'm half-asleep by the time I hear the front door close, and Kaley's cries fade in the distance.

By the time I wake up, it's dark. The house is quiet and empty, but my ears still ring with the memory of my baby's cries. I know it won't be long before Dave and Kaley will be back. I roll off the bed onto my knees and bury my face in my pillow.

Lord, please help me, I pray, *please help my daughter. I don't know what to do any more. I'm so tired. I'm so frustrated. I'm so—*I stop a moment groping for the word—*so angry.* I lift my head and rub the tears off my cheeks. *No, not angry,* I think. Furious! I am spitting-nails mad. For I've finally figured out that Kaley cries not because she has "an immature nervous system" or "neurological damage." It isn't her allergy to regular formula or a low stress level. The reason Kaley cries is because she wants her mother. She hasn't had one for so long. First her biological mother was denied her. Then the people in charge of her life, who should've known better, made it impossible for her to bond with anyone else. Those first critical months were spent mostly in the hospital. Instead of being nurtured and loved, she was tested and evaluated. How could anyone do that to a baby?

I stuff my face against the pillow again and cry, grieving for my baby and the pain and loss she suffered those first months.

Gradually my jumbled feelings and sobs turn into thoughts and words. *Father, help me with my anger. Help me to remember that I'm Your adopted child, that I belong to You. Even as I fail You . . . and myself, You love me. When I constantly cry up to You, You continue to hold me safe and comfort me. Help me love my baby, Lord, the way You love me.*

Then I return to bed, curl up under the sheet, and fall into a deep, exhausted sleep.

When I wake the next morning, the first rays of the sun lay across our bed. Dave is asleep next to me, snoring gently. Outside I hear a bird chirping; inside is complete silence.

Easing quietly out of bed, I go to Kaley's crib and look at her. She's sound asleep, completely relaxed on her back, with arms and legs outstretched in a position of surrender. Dave has put her in the yellow, terry cloth sleeper my grandmother sent.

It's getting too small already, I notice. The tips of her feet strain against the material, each small toe clearly outlined.

I think of my grandmother setting aside a little bit of her monthly check so she can give a "store-bought" present to her first great-grandchild. Grandmother did most things in little bits.

"You have to save up the little bits of good God brings your way," she told me once. "Store them in your heart— pieces of Scripture, moments of closeness with Him, things that speak of love, memories of courage. Then when trials come, the Lord calls those little bits to your mind."

"Why, Grandmother?"

"So He can put them in front of you like stepping-stones, leading you to where you need to go."

And just like that, the words in Luke come to mind as clearly as when I heard them last Easter in the Passion play.

"Father, forgive them, for they do not know what they are doing" (Luke 23:34).

I lean over the crib and tug on the sleeper around Kaley's toes, trying to stretch the material a little bit more.

"We're going to have to forgive them, Kaley," I tell her in a soft voice. "You and I. We're going to have to forgive them for hurting you. They didn't know it would hurt you so badly."

Kaley stirs, eyes fluttering, and makes sucking motions with her mouth. Something tugs at my heart. She is so beautiful! I lean closer and whisper, "I love you, Boo."

Her eyes open. When she sees me, she rolls on her stomach, makes for the side of the crib, and pulls herself up. I laugh out loud, delighted at her accomplishment. Then she greets me with a cheerful gurgle and a grin that displays four small teeth. She's beaming without a tear in sight. It is like catching a glimpse of the rainbow, promising the sun.

I take this little bit and store it in my heart.

Kaley has come such a long way from babyhood. Except for the corrective shoes she wears because of her leg, she looks like any other kindergartner. She has lost most of her baby fat and is becoming a slender, long-legged young girl. With her auburn curls smoothed into long braids, she reminds me of a miniature Pippi Longstocking, freckles and all.

She rides a yellow bus to and from school. In the mornings, we scurry around, gathering up papers, books, markers, pieces of clothing, fitting everything in her backpack, hurrying, hurrying, so we have plenty of time to wait for the school bus at the mailbox by the edge of the road. Kaley is in love with that little yellow school bus.

While I try to corral two-year-old Todd, Kaley runs up and down the road, around the mailbox, over the mailbox, around Todd and me, and back again, all the while looking for that first sign of yellow.

"Here it is," she yells. The bus stops with assorted squeals and belches. Up the steps in a flash and she is gone.

I sigh with relief, pick up Todd, and start the walk back to the house. Then I turn as I do every morning and look back one last time at the cloud of smoke that trails down the road. *Be with her, Lord,* I think, and try to push down the feelings that bubble up. I feel guilty for being grateful for those school hours that siphon some of her relentless energy.

At first Dave and I worried about Kaley starting school, because she still has a low stress tolerance and cries at a moment's notice. But she's very bright, has a terrific sense of humor, and buzzes through our days with much activity. After the first week of school, the only thing Kaley is worrying about is whether to become a teacher or a school-bus driver when she grows up.

Kaley's teacher sends home good marks on her papers and good reports with little notes that read "hard worker, curious, gets along well with others." But along with the praise comes "she's quite a handful, never sits still, is very intense."

But, all in all, she's come a long way from that baby who couldn't stop crying. I tell myself that every day. But in my heart, I know there is still something not quite right about our daughter.

She is so messy. This isn't any ordinary mess I'm talking about—but a compulsiveness. Paper in hundreds of pieces, weeks-old trash that seems to appear from nowhere, broken toys, clothes, books, just *things* everywhere. Her room can go from almost neat to wind-tunnel destruction in one day.

"So she's a messy kid," my pediatrician says when I try to tell him about it. "Set some limits. Give her some consequences. That should straighten her out." Poor parenting, he's telling me.

It isn't that simple. Everything she touches seems to end up damaged in some way. This includes herself. It seems as if there's always some part of her that has stitches or is broken or bleeding. And there are other things, too. Subtle things I can't put into words. At times I feel I have a set of twins instead of two children three years apart. Almost the same size, Todd and Kaley often act the same way, demanding the same things emotionally. I've also begun to notice that when adults talk to Kaley, she seems to rely on me to tell her what they've said, as if she can't quite understand. And then there's her brother. Rough and tumble, easygoing, calm Todd. I can't help but compare her to Todd.

Dave is taking night classes to finish his degree in criminal law enforcement, so his time with Kaley or any of us is limited to weekends. Still he's around the kids a lot.

I talk to Dave about how I feel, but he doesn't see things the way I do.

"She needs time to mature. She'll be all right," he tells me again and again. I want to believe him. Worrywart, he's telling me.

One morning a week I go to our church's Mothers' of Preschoolers program (MOPS). I love the contact with other mothers, several of whom have children with physical or emotional challenges. Next to these children Kaley looks like the "perfect" child.

"I envy you, Mary Lucy," one mother tells me when we have lunch together at McDonald's. My two children scale the playground equipment like monkeys while her child watches from a wheelchair. Any problems Kaley has seem small indeed. I let myself feel reassured.

By the end of first grade, Kaley's teacher comments that our daughter needs to settle down—"She can do better." In the mornings, after getting dressed for school, our journeys to the mailbox get slower and slower. For some reason, Kaley isn't running to catch her little yellow school bus anymore.

For the parents' conference, Mrs. Wallace, the principal of the school, arranges a special meeting with us.

Mrs. Wallace reminds me of those new grandmothers featured on some TV commercials—thoroughly modern women who look as if they bake only cookies that are low in cholesterol. Mrs. Wallace's short, silvered hair wings back perfectly.

I'm sorry now that I'm wearing blue jeans. I push my hair behind my ears, hoping to look tidier. Mrs. Wallace leans back in her desk chair and places her fingertips together.

Why didn't Dave change his boots? I think as I glance at him, but the fact that a little bit of dried mud covers the tip of his boots doesn't seem to bother him. He's concentrating on Mrs. Wallace's words.

"Clearly, Kaley's not doing her best," Mrs. Wallace is saying. "Either she has the lazy-child syndrome, or she's an underachiever. Whatever the reason, she isn't sufficiently motivated to achieve her highest."

I can't believe what I'm hearing! I think of a younger Kaley, sitting at the kitchen table, the tip of her tongue between her teeth trying so hard to color inside the lines. I think of the endless practice with her dolls, getting the diaper just right so she can help change her little brother. The most intensely curious child I've ever known, she asks questions nonstop. Kaley—an underachiever? I don't think it for a minute.

"As you can see, on the intelligence test," Mrs. Wallace says and spreads several pages in front of us, "Kaley scored very high in almost every area. Her lowest score is just above average in language development, but this could have been an off day for her. The fact is," the principal taps her pencil against the test papers for emphasis, "your daughter's overall score borders the gifted range."

"I don't understand," I manage to say.

Mrs. Wallace places another sheet of paper in front of us. "You see, on the performance test, her scores are just average with a small dip below average in speech development. Kaley is not producing the kind of work her IQ indicates she should." Mrs. Wallace lays down her pencil and leans back in her chair once more.

"So what are you suggesting?" Dave says.

"We feel that if during the summer Kaley receives extra tutoring, with a little motivation, she can bring up her performance test scores and qualify for our gifted program. Very few children qualify for this enrichment program, and since your daughter is so close . . ." The principal smiles at us with an expression akin to triumph.

"And if we don't want Kaley in the gifted program? After all you said she's a bright child doing grade-level work. Perhaps we feel this is best for her." I can't look at Dave because I can guess what he's thinking.

Mrs. Wallace frowns. "Please, Mary, let me explain. It's a

57

dog-eat-dog world out there, and we must prepare our children to compete. The sooner they learn that only the ones on top survive, the better."

Dave looks at me for a moment. I look back.

"Do you want our child to learn to eat dogs?" he asks.

"Nope," I reply.

"Neither do I."

So we leave. A few minutes later I wonder if we were too hasty. The old doubts and worries resurface. Is there something here Dave and I are missing?

After our talk with Mrs. Wallace, Dave is convinced that, no matter what the cost, we should enroll Kaley in our church's day school. We'll manage the tuition somehow. I agree reluctantly. I'm not sure changing schools is all that good for Kaley.

"What we decide now for her," Dave tells me, "will make or break her." The picture of my daughter "breaking" chills my heart.

I'm relieved when Kaley tells me she loves her second-grade teacher. "We talk about Jesus every day, Mom. *And* we pray for people." With a happy heart I sign up Todd for kindergarten.

Toward the end of second grade, however, Kaley's grades fall suddenly. When she gets home, she either cries and whines the whole evening or is so worn out she falls asleep at the dinner table. Finally, even Dave has to admit something is wrong. On the advice of her teacher we go back to Children's Hospital. At the developmental center there, we have Kaley tested.

The psychologist who led the testing team gets right to the point. "Kaley shows marked difficulties in visual-motor and auditory-motor integration and expression. She also shows body asymmetry and confusion in left-right dominance. Expression of complex ideas are just beyond her reach. Abstract thinking is difficult for her to express in a comprehensive whole."

I shake my head in confusion. I feel disoriented as if I have made a trip in a time machine.

There's something wrong with her, there's something wrong with her. Pay attention, I tell you, there's something wrong with her.

"What does all of this mean?" I ask.

"In practical terms she has difficulty reading or writing, copying from the board, following more than two instructions at a time, or expressing her ideas well enough to be understood."

"But we were told just a year ago that Kaley tested as a gifted child with a high IQ." I can hear the frustration in Dave's voice. And the pain.

I feel numb.

"Kaley has the invisible handicap of learning disabilities. Fortunately for her, she is also very intelligent. You must realize that being learning disabled is not a measure of retardation or IQ. It simply means that learning needs to happen in a different way than for most people."

"When you said 'difficult,' exactly what does that mean?" I ask.

"Unfortunately, there aren't any exact answers in Kaley's case." The psychologist sighs and looks at us with kindness in her eyes. "You might compare her problem to the kind of brain damage a stroke victim suffers. Except the term *brain damage* is misleading. The term *Minimal Brain Dysfunction* is preferred, because the problem is with brain function, not the brain itself. The circuits of the brain appear to be connected or to function differently."

We all three sit in silence for a moment. I find I can't talk, I can't think. Dave asks, "Is there help for her?"

"If you're asking if the problem can be eliminated—no. There's not much available in the way of treatment. Yet each child should be dealt with as an individual. There is no way of knowing how much she can learn by compensating. Also, the question remains open whether or not she will be able to function in a normal classroom setting."

I don't want to believe what I'm hearing. I want to put my hands over my ears, squeeze my eyes shut, and whistle a

song so I don't have to hear. But I can't block it out. It's true
... what I've feared all along is really true. *There's something
wrong with her.* I avoid looking at Dave. Right now I don't
want to see his eyes and the hurt and the anger.

After the numbness has worn off, I must admit I feel happy.
Yes, happy. Happy and relieved that Kaley doesn't have a brain
tumor, that I'm not a "bad" mother, that I'm not imagining
things or going crazy.

"It explains so much," I tell Dave. "M★A★S★H," our favorite TV show, is on, but I can tell he's not watching it. There
are tears glistening in his eyes, and I can see the moving figures
on the screen reflected in them.

"I can't believe that God would give up on Kaley after
He's brought her so far," Dave says abruptly. "She's going to
be all right. Just watch and see." He pulls me close and I can
smell the out-of-doors in his shirt.

Suddenly, without warning, I feel a terrible jolt, an in-
credible sense of sadness and loss that is as painful as if something physically was tearing inside of me.

I remember, when we first brought Kaley home, I thought
warmth and security would make Kaley whole again. I was
convinced that our love for her would be enough to heal all
of her hurts.

I put my face against Dave's shirt and cry for a long time.

When I read my Bible that night, there's a verse in Psalms
that touches my heart.

"My soul is weary with sorrow; strengthen me according
to your word" (Psalm 119:28).

That fall Kaley begins third grade. Right away it's obvious
to us that reading, writing, and independent work are more
vital in the third grade than they were in the lower grades.
We're hoping that the church school's small class size and
the extra help we give her at home will be enough. It isn't.

"Mommy, am I retarded?" Kaley asks me one day out of
the blue. Abruptly, I stop the sewing machine, my heart in
my throat. *Oh, no,* I think, *I knew this was coming—and,*

wouldn't you know it, the timing is lousy. I have less than 30 minutes to complete her costume for the Christmas pageant.

On the other hand, I tell myself, *the timing will always be lousy.* With a sigh I slide the white, frothy material aside and turn to get a good look at my daughter. She's chewing thoughtfully on a long strand of the burnished copper hair that flows down her back. Overall she seems calm and unconcerned, as if all eight-year-olds ask their mothers if they are retarded. But when she looks up, her blue eyes are open wide, and frown lines pull across her forehead.

Pain shoots through me. I turn quickly toward the sewing machine, not wanting to take the chance that my reaction shows on my face. The intensity of my feelings surprises me. Feelings of hurt and reluctance . . . and, in a strange way, relief. My knee hits one of the table's spindle legs, and tears film my eyes. With care I slip the edge of the costume in place and lower the needle foot on the sewing machine.

Now what, Lord? I think, sending up a little mental telegram. *How do I tell her she's less than perfect?*

"What made you ask that question, Boo?" I finally say, trying to sound casual. I use her old nickname on purpose, hoping it will bring comfort . . . needing that comfort myself.

"When I got to Melissa's, she says . . ." I look over my shoulder at Kaley. She has placed her hands on her hips and is scrunching her face in a pretty good imitation of her best friend, Melissa.

"Melissa says to me, 'Kaley, you're so dumb you're retarded,' and the other girls go, 'Yea, you're a reeeetard—reeeetard.' "

"Oh, Boo," I say, my heart full of sympathy. "What did you say?"

"I didn't say anything. I just turned and left," she says, rolling her eyes in a gesture of scorn. "They're the ones retarded." She adds a snort of disgust. Then her face changes, serious once more, and she steps closer to me.

"Why would they say that, Mom?"

I put my arm around Kaley's slender waist, pull her closer,

and look up at her. "I'm sorry, Boo. Those girls were being very unkind."

"Oh," she says, seemingly without emotion, "then I'm not retarded, am I?"

"No, you're not."

"But I am different." The wrinkles return to her forehead, and a hurt and puzzled expression comes over her face. "Why can't I be like other kids? Why did God make me so dumb?"

She stares straight into my eyes for a long moment. Her deep-set almond-shaped eyes are so clear and so full of trust. I catch my breath in wonder.

I'm reminded of teacup roses, and little yellow school buses, and other little bits of good.

I take a breath and say, "Did I ever tell you about the time I asked my grandmother just about the same thing?"

"Grandmother Blackwell? The one who raised you?"

"That's right, and I was just about your age, too." Kaley settles on her knees and rests her arms in my lap, ready to listen.

"It was the first day of school, if I remember correctly, and I was wearing a new dress with a wide sash that tied into a large puff bow in the back. I think it was blue, with smocking on the front that Grandmother had done by hand."

"You thought you were dumb?" Kaley prompts me.

"No, I thought I was ugly! Actually, I didn't start the day off thinking that, but by the end of the day, I was completely convinced of it. One of the older girls in school told me it was too bad my face didn't match my dress—it was pretty, but I was ugly."

"Ugly?" Kaley wrinkles her nose in disbelief.

"It caught on fast around school. The boys chanted ug—ug—ug when they saw me."

"That's disgusting." Kaley says in an offended tone. "What did Grandmother say?"

"Mary Lucy, pretty is as pretty does."

"Is that all?"

"Then she handed me a mirror and said, 'See what God has fearfully and wonderfully made.' "

"I bet I know what you saw in the mirror," Kaley states.

"What?"

"The prettiest mom in the whole world!"

In school today Kaley's teacher crumpled her papers and threw them in the trash because they were "unreadable." Kaley is falling further behind day by day. When I talk to the teacher about Kaley's special needs, he refuses to believe me. "She looks and acts normal enough," he declares. "I think she doesn't understand because she doesn't *want* to understand. Not because she can't. You baby her." Overprotective mother, he's telling me.

In a way I can't blame him for thinking that way. I still have trouble realizing the extent of Kaley's problems myself. But soon one hour's worth of homework stretches through the whole evening. She seems totally reliant on me to "translate" everything into simpler words and concepts so she can understand. But I can't be with her in the classroom. Oh, God, I can't be with her for the rest of her life.

We decide to confront the principal with our frustration. He is sympathetic but not very helpful.

"You have to remember we're a church school, Mary Lucy. We would like to help Kaley, but our resources are severely limited. We're not trained or equipped to deal with children who have problems. It's impossible to have Kaley in the classroom if she can't keep up with the other children. Perhaps you should look into the special education program in the public school."

I can't decide whether to slap him or beat him over the head. How dare his school be so inadequate! Why can't the teachers learn to teach all children? Do only "perfect" children rate a Christian education? I want someone to take responsibility, someone to take the blame. But getting raging mad at the school and the teachers doesn't help. When the anger is gone there's nothing left but raw frustration.

The psychologist talked about treatment and "compensating." Somehow we have to get her help. But how? No one we know understands how to help a gifted child with a learning disability. We certainly don't.

When Dave and I grew up, if people weren't mentally retarded, they were considered "normal." The world accepted three categories for "normal" people—smart, average, or dumb. Although we encountered plenty of "dumb" people, we didn't know anything about learning disabilities—much less have personal contact with a near-genius who can barely write her own name. Kaley is locked inside a super brain, unable to make herself clearly understood. But she knows what a prison that makes for her. Is there a place in the system for a person like that ... a person like Kaley?

With sinking hearts we take Kaley out of our church's school and enroll her back at her old public school so she can be evaluated for special education.

Mrs. Wallace won't accept our independent testing, because "the school district can only legally recognize their own screening test." So Kaley is tested once more.

"I tried my best, Mom. I think I did real good." And so she did. Her test results are on the edge of ineligibility according to the guidelines set by the state. Kaley doesn't qualify for help.

"At this time," Mrs. Wallace tells us, every hair still perfectly in place, "Kaley doesn't qualify. A few years from now, without help, she should be sufficiently behind to qualify for special education." Too exhausted for anger, I burst into tears outside her office.

Kaley continues in public school with outside tutoring and counseling but, by the end of the fourth grade, we feel as if we no longer have the same daughter. There are tremendous changes in Kaley. The right answers she knows in her head become wrong answers on her test papers. And she can't understand why. Soon she refuses to do any homework or study at all. Once outgoing and friendly, she now hangs back from playing with other kids her age. She still is close to Todd but blames him for everything and is quick to pick a fight with him.

She has always been a picky eater; now she refuses to eat most things I fix. She's losing weight and has headaches and stomachaches. She has crying spells and angry outbursts over the smallest things. Moody and withdrawn, she barely gets through the day without calling to say she's sick and wants to come home.

"Everyone hates me," she complains, "and so I hate them, too."

"Hey, Boo, what happened to that sunny, little girl who wanted to drive a little yellow school bus?" I tease her gently.

"She's dead."

Back-to-school preparations begin for the fifth grade. Kaley still doesn't qualify for special education. For some reason I'm gratified, but what now? What are we going to do?

"You teach me," Kaley pleads. "We can have school at home."

Frankly, the same solution has occurred to me. Home school is a hot topic in parents' group, a bunch of parents I met years ago through MOPS. We get together twice a month to share our struggles and pray for the kids we have who are in "crisis."

One mother is actually making home school work. The news broadcasts are full of parents who feel it is the only way to go. Of course, these parents usually tell their story from prison, since home schooling is illegal in our state.

Can I teach Kaley at home and give her the education she needs? Will I break the law for her sake? I'm tempted. But the minute Kaley pleads with me I realize I can't give her the special help she requires. She's already too dependent on me. Staying home is the wrong choice for her. But our choices are running out.

About the only positive thing in Kaley's life right now is that she loves her tutoring at a special facility recommended by the developmental center. All I know about this school is that it's small and very expensive, dealing with children who are "different" somehow.

The school is located on a five-acre shotgun lot in the middle of an exclusive residential neighborhood. I think the place looks more like someone's mistaken idea of a day camp than a school. A hodgepodge of aluminum buildings sits on the first half-acre, then stretches back to include horse corrals, stables, riding arenas, trees, and more trees. Each week while I wait for Kaley, I park my little Volkswagen alongside the Mercedes and Volvos and watch the squirrels scold each other. Bambi, a tame deer, wanders in and around the grove of trees, sometimes disturbing a family of ducks, sending the mother duck quacking like crazy.

It's nice being here, but once-a-week tutoring for 30 minutes is like getting a Snoopy Band-Aid for a serious injury. You're just fooled into thinking it feels better.

Dave and I talk all the time about the possibility of sending Kaley to some sort of private school, where she can get a lot of one-on-one attention. Most of the programs we've looked at dealt with children who have severe emotional and behavioral problems. The cost of tuition is out of sight, so high it's completely unrealistic.

In our parents' group, we often talk about the issue of specialty schools. Our circle of parents, who I think are more informed than most of the educational experts we consulted, divides loosely into two sides, each offering opposite advice.

One side has a "sink or swim" approach. Let Kaley grow up as is, in the "real world." She'll learn to survive, they say. Kids are tough. She will develop compensatory skills and be stronger for it. The hothouse atmosphere of a special school will be the worst thing for her. Everyone knows what happens when a hothouse plant is taken out of its protective environment—it dies. You can't expect to protect Kaley forever, they point out.

However, parents with the opposite viewpoint tell us that if Kaley remains in a regular school system she is doomed. Like a fragile flower, she needs time to develop deep roots. Place her in a learning situation that will strengthen her. The encouragement she receives and the skills she learns will enable her to survive in the "real" world later.

The group argues the issue for an hour or longer. I can't take it anymore. No one agrees on anything, knows anything, or even understands how devastated I feel. It's just too hard to make decisions that will affect Kaley for a lifetime.

It's Dave's turn to read the Scripture selection tonight. It's somewhere in Chronicles, but I'm too distraught to listen. Despite myself I hear a few words here and there.

"Do not be afraid or discouraged.... For the battle is not yours, but God's.... You will not have to fight this battle. Take up your positions; stand firm and see the deliverance the Lord will give you.... Go out to face them tomorrow, and the Lord will be with you" (2 Chronicles 2:15, 17).

When we all pray together, my prayer is this: "Lord, if You'll show me the position You want me to take, with Your help, I'll try to stand firm. But," I add, "I'm not promising anything."

It's a good thing He loves me.

The next Monday I talk to Mrs. Findell, the director and owner of the school where Kaley gets tutoring. She knows Kaley's history.

"Like your daughter, most of the children who attend this school have slipped through the cracks of other school systems," she says. "Their learning difficulties are either not considered severe enough to warrant intervention or are simply not recognized as such by educators. Most of these children end up labeled as behavioral problems."

She shows me around the grounds, explaining the different programs offered. I hate to admit it, but I'm impressed.

In one classroom, Emily, who looks about 10, puts down the book she's reading, *War and Peace,* so that another child can help her with division.

In the next room, Max, a kindergartner, in halting words describes his show-and-tell. It's the first complete sentence he has ever spoken, the director tells me. However, in math Max is adding and subtracting two-column figures. "We work on the weaknesses," Mrs. Findell says, "but we also build on strengths, encouraging each child to go as far as possible in his or her strong area."

The scars covering a large part of Ashley's body testify to long hospital stays and missed school. In a regular school she would be held back a grade to catch up. Here she's with her peers, learning at her own level. "Don't worry, she'll be on grade level by the time she graduates," Mrs. Findell says in response to the look on my face. Ashley giggles and runs to play cheerleader with her friends.

Fifteen-year-old Sally reads to a group of first graders from a third-grade book. The kids love their "teacher." They don't know this is the first book the teenager has been able to read from cover to cover. They clap when she finishes. Sally beams.

"These children are all regular kids," Mrs. Findell elaborates. "Most have high IQs and only minor physical anomalies." I raised my eyebrows in question. "Like your Kaley's bone deformity. Very slight and usually unnoticeable. This is not the school for children with marked retardation or major physical handicaps. They attend other facilities. Our kids are those who have no other place to go."

It sounds so good. Still, as I listen to her, I wonder. How many of the niceties are to impress the parents? Everywhere I look I see teachers wearing blue jeans and sandals, kids in cutoffs. Everything has such a casual air. How much can Kaley really learn here? Do we want our daughter separated from the mainstream of society like this? If she goes here she'll definitely be labeled "different." I want help for her—not to be marked for life.

But I swallow my misgivings. We have to at least try it. Kaley simply has no other place to go.

We scrape together enough money for the first two months of tuition, and I start looking for a way to earn some extra money. The tuition is not as high as most of the other "specialty" schools, but definitely is not within our current means. Dave and I are both determined that if this is what Kaley needs, God will help us find a way.

The first time Kaley takes a test at her new school, half

of the answers she writes are either illegible or wrong. Her teacher calls her aside.

"Kaley, I know you studied. I bet you could tell me all the right answers to these questions." She can and does. She makes an A on the test.

Soon Monday mornings come without complaints, stomachaches, or pleas to stay home. With shorter school days (five hours a day with three hours on Friday), Kaley is able to participate in other activities. Dave takes her to swim-team practice three times a week. It gives her the gross motor patterning she needs. Through the school I find a piano teacher with an educational background in learning disabilities, and Kaley begins the music lessons that help her eye/hand coordination. Instead of long hours trying to complete homework, she improves her social skills, playing with new friends. Even her relationship with her brother improves.

Kaley is blossoming. Her two-year developmental lag isn't noticeable among her fellow late bloomers. Soon the house is full of laughing girls, and the phone rings off the hook with boys calling.

I consider doing day care in my home to pay for tuition, but then, just like a gift, Mrs. Findell asks me to be the teaching assistant for the kindergarten class in exchange for tuition. My heart sings!

By the end of Kaley's first year in her special school, it's obvious to everyone that this is the place for her.

"Kaley, what do you like about going to your school?" I ask her one day.

She thinks for a moment, frown lines gathering in concentration between her blue eyes. "I guess the best thing is everyone likes me," she says finally.

"How do you know that?"

"I have a nickname! My friends gave it to me."

"Wait, don't tell me, let me guess. They call you Boo."

She laughs. "No, they call me Sunny." She flashes a smile at me. "You know—as in sunshine!" And with that she is out the door, long red hair streaming behind her.

I was so afraid that Kaley would feel "different." Instead, for the first time in her life, she belongs.

An Encouraging Word

Mary Lucy's pain and struggle with her adopted daughter's defects are very real. What courage it takes to adopt a special-needs child! What energy it takes to pour all of one's self into seeing a child survive, grow, bloom in a world that might push her aside as defective and unimportant. Seeing Kaley eventually begin to blossom and shine brings tears to one's eyes.

Hats Off to Adoptive Parents!

Hats off to Mary Lucy and to all parents like her who love a less-than-perfect child! And, hats off to Mary Lucy and Dave's exceptional marriage relationship. For this woman and her husband, such an adoption is truly a joint venture. Dave is there every step of the way, sharing the laughter and the tears, easing the burden for both Mary and Kaley. Such supportive, caring men are hard to find. Early in Kaley's life, Mary Lucy's internal resources are depleted, and she is having difficulty coping with Kaley's crying, Dave takes the baby from her arms. Mary Lucy doesn't tell us where Dave went or what he did, but we do know the effect it has on Mary Lucy. It gave her a chance to gather her strength, to talk to her heavenly Father, and to regroup so that she could continue in her persistent quest to mother this restless, taut infant.

When a special-needs child is first adopted as an infant, the task does not seem to be such an all-consuming project. Babies and young children often have a fresh and new look. Most of them, even ones who cry a lot, look and act very much like other infants. A mother invests a special feeling of hope and potential in the squirming bit of new life she holds in her arms.

Most parents look at the tiny infant and plan for the day when that child will go to kindergarten, high school, and maybe even college. Some parents envision their baby as almost a hero, the one in the family who might raise the image of the mother or the entire family in the eyes of the community. How natural for parents to begin saying to a young child, "You can be whatever you want to be—doctor, lawyer, merchant, chief."

The mother of the special-needs child is no different. She sees her child as wonderful, a special gift from God. At first, she may feel that all the child needs is her love and her care, which Mary Lucy gave Kaley in a touching and beautiful manner. Those early years of mothering include the important phase of bonding, when every mother gives the infant her hopes, her dreams, her faith. The tiny child learns to trust this adult called "mama." As time continues, the child takes on the values and ideals of mom. The child wants to please her and will work very hard to do so. The mother and the child are almost one, almost indistinguishable at times. The mother feels what the child feels and comforts her young with touching, cooing, feeding, and diapering.

Reality Sets In

Somewhere along the line, all mothers feel the cold, hard dash of reality: their child is only one among many, unique, but probably not outstanding. Slowly, every mother begins to get in touch with her child's strengths and weaknesses. The child gets an A in this subject under these circumstances and a C or D in another subject in a different environment. Some children begin excelling in sports; others practice and practice, yet don't make the team. Gradually, the child's identity emerges, and her self-confidence and self-esteem develop and somehow stay intact, assuming she fits the norms of society.

The experience of the special-needs mother, however, is an entirely different matter. She begins to know early on there are things that make her child different, things that prevent her child from fitting in. It becomes evident, especially in the first few years of school, that her child is ending up at the bottom of the heap in the competitive world of the elementary school system. Reality hits the parent of a special-needs child squarely in the face.

Special-Needs Parents Face Criticism

Often the reality comes in the form of criticism of one's parenting techniques, even though the criticizer knows nothing of what the dedicated, skilled, and hard-working parent of the special-needs child is doing. People will go so far as to say directly to the parent's face that she is not strict enough or is faulty in some other way. Teachers may view the child as looking too "normal" or too cute to have a serious problem: "She's just spoiled/immature and will grow out of it." Even many trained family therapists will work long and hard to help change the mother's and father's parenting techniques— unless the therapist thinks to call for the child to be tested for internal deficits in the brain or in the way the brain is connected to the input or output capacities, as in dyslexic or other learning-disabled children. Nor should supportive friends automatically be expected to help. Few adults understand special-needs children and how to cope with them. Some people, like the M.D. and the principal in Kaley's case, only enable the parents to avoid facing the truth.

Denial is probably the easiest way to deal with the whole situation, but it is not helpful. Grasping at straws won't work either. Even though the child may be getting failing grades in everything, along with bad conduct reports, she may exhibit one exceptional skill (such as playing the piano by ear)—an anomaly the parent grasps as sure hope that the child will be okay.

Where to Begin

When a parent comes to realize and accept the fact that she has a seriously impaired child, she, like Mary Lucy, can begin to take action.

The first step is to define the problem. Many parents can do this themselves by keeping a log of the good and bad days the child has and by recording the events of the day as well as the behavior of the child. A pattern of behavior usually emerges, which helps the parent begin to arrange the environment in order to compensate for the child's deficits. Mary Lucy did this when she learned the feeding schedule of Kaley in those early weeks and months of parenting.

It is also essential that the child be tested by a trained psychologist and a neurologist. The former specializes in diagnosing learning disabilities and in detecting symptoms for hyperactivity. A neurologist provides additional testing, defining more specifically any discernable brain damage. From reading the story of Kaley, an expert would assume that Kaley has Attention Deficit Disorder (ADD). Some children have this disorder with hyperactivity (ADHD). The criteria for a medical diagnosis of ADHD are as follows:

1. A disturbance of at least six months during which at least eight of the following are present:

☐ Often fidgets with hands or feet or squirms in seat (in adolescents, may be limited to subjective feelings of restlessness)

☐ Has difficulty remaining seated when required to do so

☐ Is easily distracted by external stimuli

☐ Has difficulty awaiting turn in games or group situations

☐ Often blurts out answers to questions before they have been completed

☐ Has difficulty following through on instructions from others (not due to oppositional behavior or failure of comprehension); e.g., fails to finish chores

☐ Has difficulty sustaining attention in tasks or play activities

☐ Often shifts from one unfinished activity to another

☐ Has difficulty playing quietly

☐ Often talks excessively

☐ Often interrupts or intrudes on others; e.g., butts into other children's games

☐ Often does not seem to listen to what is being said to him or her

☐ Often loses things necessary for tasks or activities at school or at home (e.g., toys, pencils, books, assignments)

☐ Often engages in physically dangerous activities without considering possible consequences (not for the purpose of thrill seeking); e.g., runs into street without looking

Note: The above items are listed in descending order of discriminating power based on data from a national field trial of the DSM-III-R criteria for Disruptive Behavior Disorders.
2. Onset before the age of seven (*Diagnostic and Statistical Manual of Mental Disorders.* 3d rev. ed. DSM-III-R. Washington, D.C.: American Psychiatric Association, 1987, pp. 52–53).

The disorder occurs three to nine times more frequently in males than in females.

What If You're Not Sure?
A mother who suspects her child might have the diagnosis of ADD should check with an expert in the field of child psychiatry, as there are other disorders that are very similar to ADD.

As Mary Lucy points out in her story, associated features of an ADHD child include low self-esteem, mood shifts, frustration, and temper.

Today there is extensive testing available that can pinpoint specifically how, what, when, and where an individual child can reach her maximum learning potential. Psychologists and neurologists can point out specific strengths, weaknesses, and learning styles of each student. The testing can be helpful long before the child fails so miserably in school that he or she is no longer able to participate in a regular, mainstream classroom. As happened in Kaley's case, tutoring and even a specialized school might be helpful before the child is actually labeled as learning disabled or emotionally handicapped.

How much Kaley will be able to learn or how far she might be able to go with her education is not certain. However, Kaley is in a school setting that recognizes her uniqueness and maximizes her learning potential, a setting in which she can learn with high self-esteem and an acceptable level of success. What a blessing for little Kaley Rose that her mother grappled with the reality of the problem, searched, prayed, and found an excellent school to help Kaley through this difficult stage of her life!

What will happen next to Kaley? Will she outgrow some of her Attention Deficit Disorder problem? Will she forever have a problem with learning the conventional way? Such prediction is difficult because of the many variables in her life. In all probability, Kaley will always need a controlled environment for top productivity. She may not have the options an average adult has; however, she will have options. One would hope that she will begin to know her strengths and her learning style, that she will begin to gravitate toward the things that work for her, and that she will learn how to create an environment for herself that will allow her to be a functional, productive member of society.

Could You Mother a Special-Needs Child?

How does a woman know if she has what it takes to be the mother of a special-needs child?

Look back at Mary Lucy and analyze the characteristics that have enabled her to succeed at this endeavor. She appears to be a mentally healthy, well-integrated individual with a good social support system and a strong faith in God.

She is sensitive. She is aware of her own feelings and the feelings of others. She expresses her feelings to others.

She has a support system to give her relief. She has her husband, a mothers' support group, and a parenting support group.

She has the ability to bond.

She is willing to depend on God.

She has deep roots and stability.

She is not afraid of reality.

She uses the knowledge of specialists trained in the field.

There are many special-needs children available for adoption today. Some are very much like Kaley, while others are quite different. Some are physically handicapped or intellectually handicapped. Others are handicapped because a parent was addicted to drugs. Still others are labeled as special-needs children only because their race leaves them in the unwanted category.

Many more adoptive parents with some of Mary Lucy's characteristics are needed in order to care for special-needs children. Traditional, two-parent families are not the only ones capable of being successful with special-needs children. Single parents and older couples who have already raised their children are also helping care for special-needs children like Kaley.

It is through the work and patience of mothers like Mary Lucy that children like Kaley can grow up and discover that the world does not have to be a hostile place after all. The world can be a trustworthy place where God's patient understanding and just the right help make the hurt go away.

Blossom, Sunny. God loves you, and mother is there.

Shirley Schaper

Reflection

- What kinds of emotions did Mary Lucy experience throughout the story? Have you ever felt as she did?

- Whose adopted child are you? Read Ephesians 1:4–6; Romans 8:23; and Galatians 3:26–29.

- Do you have "little bits of good" stored in your heart? What does God say to write in your heart? Read Proverbs 3:3; 2 Corinthians 3:2–3; Proverbs 2:1–10.

- In what ways are you "less than perfect?" How does your heavenly Father see you? Read Galatians 5:17–18; Romans 8:1–2; Galatians 5:22—23; and 1 John 1:9.

- How do you show the children in your life (the children you care about) your unconditional love?

- What advantage do you see in parents sharing common problems, listening, and supporting one another in their parenting roles?

- Consider getting together with one or two other parents to share, pray for your children, and discuss solutions to common problems.

Dear Father,
Sometimes
I feel so small
And helpless,
Just like a tiny child.

It's so hard
To puzzle out the pieces
Of life
And understand what's going on.

You understand, though.
You, Father, know my fears.
You listen to my rage.
You see my tears.
You share my relief and my laughter.

You understand
This fierce love I have
For my child,
Because You are a parent, too.

Hold us both,
My child and me,
In the palm of Your gentle hand,
And mother us
As You already have
Until it all comes clear.

Amen.

A Word to Mothers of Children with ADD

You probably have been concerned about your child for sometime. Maybe he's the class clown, getting into trouble all the time, even to the extent of being kicked out of class. Or perhaps he avoids activities. "It's too boring" or "I just don't want to" he'll say and seems to be developing a passive approach to everything.

Sometimes you worry that you'll be suspected of child abuse because your child always seems to be covered with bruises, cuts, bumps from running into and falling from things. He was late in learning how to ride a bike, jump rope, and kick a ball.

It could be your child does poorly in games and sports played by his peers and prefers instead to play with children much younger than he. He can't do his homework without constant supervision from you. When you talk to him, he doesn't "tune in" until you're well into your third paragraph.

Parent-teacher conferences are becoming increasingly disturbing—even alarming and frustrating. His teachers may say his poor class work is due to laziness, daydreaming, emotional impairment, stubbornness, or mental dullness.

He gets backaches, headaches, stomachaches, or pain in his hands or legs when he wakes on school mornings. But when you let him stay home, he's well by midmorning. His failures are never his fault. It's your fault or the teacher's or the other boy's.

When you talk to your pediatrician about the problems, the doctor says something like "boys will be boys" or "he's just going through a phase." Maybe you are beginning to feel that somehow you are responsible for your child's overactive aggressiveness, inattention, and scholastic inadequacies.

He's always on the "go" and acts as if "driven." One minute he bursts out with uncontrolled anger; the next minute he cries because he thinks he's been picked on.

You're beginning to hate the child you love so much. Either he's impulsive and destructive, or he's kind, showing a rich imagination and unique creativity.

There's also a 20 percent chance your child is adopted. He probably has one or more minor physical anomalies, increased incidence of allergies, bed wetting, upper respiratory and middle ear infections.

But you can't quite figure it out. All you know is this: there's something wrong with my child.

What You Can Do

1. Have a complete evaluation of your child—medical studies, psychological and educational testing, speech and language assessment, neurological evaluation, and behavioral rating scales. In most states, your public school system is required to provide the testing as described above—even if the student attends a private school. It's free. It's your child's right. Insist on it.

2. Remember that ADD is not a form of mental retardation, emotional or mental illness. The emotional problems these children have do not cause the academic difficulties; the academic difficulties cause the emotional problems.

3. You can learn to be assertive in getting what your child needs. Work to get an individualized approach. Educate his teachers. Run interference as much as possible.

4. Be aware that not all doctors, psychologists, social workers, teachers, or professionals in the mental health disciplines are experts in the area of learning disabilities and/or Attention Deficit Disorder. Search until you find a support team of experts that are. Consult with them often.

5. Keep yourself spiritually fit. Small Bible studies and church support groups are invaluable. Develop prayer partners who will support you in daily prayer.

6. Don't forget you and your child are not alone. The Lord is with you every step of the way. "My grace is sufficient for you, for my power is made perfect in weakness" (2 Corinthians 12:9).
7. Learn all you can about your child and every aspect of ADD and related conditions.

There are many books and pamphlets available. For *Coping with Your Inattentive Child; Attention Deficit Disorder in Teenagers and Young Adults;* and many other valuable resources for parents and teachers, write to Minerva Press, 6653 Andersonville Road, Waterford, MI 48095.

Information is also available from the Attention Deficit Disorder Advocacy Group (ADDAG), 8091 South Ireland Way, Aurora, CO 80016 (phone 303/690-7548).

Additional Recommended Reading

Brutten, Milton, Sylvia O. Richardson, and Charles Mangel. *Something's Wrong with My Child.* New York: Harcourt Brace Jovanovich, 1979.

Silver, Larry B., M.D. *Attention Deficit Disorder: A Booklet for Parents.* Summit, NJ: Ciba Corp., 1987. (For information write to Ciba Corp., 556 Morris Ave., Summit, NJ 07901.)

Weiss, Helen Ginandes, and Martin S. Weiss. *Home Is a Learning Place: A Parents Guide to Learning Disabilities.* Boston: Little Brown and Co., 1976.

Kristl Franklin

Kesi: Through a Glass Darkly

by Nikki Rochester

Kesi

KESI

The mind has a way of photographing moments in our lives and stashing the pictures neatly away in an album of indelible memories. Somehow the mind appreciates, long before we, the critical significance of those moments. You never have to leaf through the album. The photos are mysteriously called to mind whenever they are needed: sometimes to warn, sometimes to humble, sometimes to cheer.

This is one of those moments. Some anonymous clinician just told my 18-year-old daughter that she is seven weeks pregnant. I practically felt my mind snap the picture. My face had to be as blank and expressionless as my heart. I had expected to feel angry, maybe even a little hysterical. Yet, I love my child, but right now I don't even feel like hugging her. In fact, I don't feel anything! I had asked God to spare us this trial, but I have no choice but to accept His answer in the words of this physician. I suppose, in a sense, the numbness is a blessing.

The doctor is talking to both of us about prenatal care and other important details that I should be listening to, but I am totally engrossed in scrutinizing my daughter. I had poured into her everything I believed in, everything I stood for. She was supposed to reap the benefits of everything generations of people had struggled for. And here she sat in a maternity clinic, becoming one of those despicable statistics she had been groomed to rise above.

It's funny. Though my husband, Evan, died nine years ago, I rarely think of myself as a widow. I realize the term is merely a marital status label. But for me it conjures up images of a woman in mourning, focusing on what was. Ordinarily, my life is nothing like that. Ordinarily, I choose to remember with joy what was but to focus on the now. But today is not an ordinary day. Today I feel like a widow.

Evan and I were like storybook characters. We grew up in the same neighborhood. Our families attended the same church. We played together in elementary school, despised each other in junior high, and dated each other in high school. He graduated from high school two years ahead of me and went out of state to college. That's when I realized how special he was to me. By the time I started college, we were in love. When I graduated from college, we got married.

We were an idealistic pair, a product of the sixties who took our causes seriously. And the cause to which we were the most passionately committed was the black liberation movement. During our college years, we had each undergone a slow, traumatic, and painful correction of vision. Little by little, we learned enough history to be convinced that we are an accomplished and capable race. And we studied enough of the world's diverse cultures to acquire a broader, more self-affirming perspective of life. Those painstaking and precious lessons radically altered the course of our lives.

We had always been taught, both in subtle and overt ways, that "black" (the lifestyle, the look, the lingo) was second rate, the absolute antithesis of success. And the ticket out, up and away from "second rate" to "success" was education. With the right credentials, you could overcome and renounce any counterproductive ethnic ties. But by the time Evan and I got our "tickets," we'd been transformed. We didn't want to escape from our community. We wanted to embrace it and build it.

It was an exciting and absorbing passion for us. Every decision we made—which job to take, what car to buy, where to buy it, which magazines to subscribe to, even the movies and restaurants we patronized—reflected that central commitment. I stopped straightening my hair in affirmation of its natural texture. I went so far as to legally drop my "slave name" (Shannon) and choose an African name with a meaning

86

I could appreciate. Kesi means "born when father was in trouble." It was my way of saying that this new ethnic identity of mine was "born" as a result of the "trouble" black people, as symbolized by the men or the fathers, were in. Evan, on the other hand, chose to keep his given name, because he contended that everything he did invested his name with meaning! That's the way it was with us. We believed in the same values and principles, but we each had our own way of living out that faith.

We had been married about two years when I got pregnant. Evan was ecstatic. To him, a baby was yet another means of infusing fresh values into our community. For me, just becoming a mother was excitement and trepidation enough, never mind the socio-political implications of the matter! Ironically, it was Evan who spent weeks researching the African name books for a name for our child. Every few days, he would come up with a possibility and solicit my opinion, and we would have long discussions about each name. By the time I was due to deliver, we had narrowed it down to Damany (which means "thinker") for a boy or Adisa (which means "makes his meaning clear") for a girl. If we gave birth to Damany, we wanted him to think for himself and not be a mindless follower of crowds. And if we gave birth to Adisa, we wanted her to use all the wisdom we would instill in her to communicate a liberated mindset to her peers.

God not only chose to entrust to us a healthy and beautiful Adisa, but He used the experience to bring us back to Him. Both Evan and I had drifted away from regular churchgoing during our college years. For me, it was a lapse that grew out of being away from home and my home church. Whenever I was at home, I was comfortable about going and enjoyed the reunion. Evan, however, had begun to distance himself from church on principle. He insisted that the churches he visited were more often instruments of oppression rather than the tools of liberation they were meant to be. Of course, we were married in our home church and would often join our families there on special occasions. Each of us professed to have faith in God, but I doubt if either of us realized how utterly malnourished and atrophied our faiths had become.

I'm not certain how or why, but during my pregnancy that deficit became more apparent to me. Maybe being a part of God's process of creation pricks at quenched spirits, but I just felt the need to go to church. I talked to Evan about it, because I thought it was something we should do together. He encouraged me to go and fulfill my need. (I think Evan thought it was just another craving of a pregnant woman!) I began to attend regularly, but Evan insisted that it "just wasn't there" for him. After Adisa was born, I continued to go and became even more involved in classes and activities. Evan was both surprised and curious. He began making occasional visits. Next he volunteered to work with another man who wanted to start a prison ministry at the church. Then he started participating in a Bible class for the prison ministry workers. And it went uphill from there. God molded Evan into a deeply spiritual man.

That long procession of thoughts and memories is parading through my mind as I look at my daughter now, 18 years later. The very fact that we are sitting in this clinic seems like a betrayal of all those dear memories. And I am quietly but profoundly devastated.

I am accustomed to reading Adisa's face and body language, but right now they aren't telling me anything about what's going on inside her. What is she feeling? What is she thinking? How much could she possibly know about the road that lies ahead of her?

ADISA

I think it's kind of ironic to feel so empty about being told you're pregnant. I feel empty, and sad I guess, but I can't get over how calm I feel. Of course, I know only too well that panicking does not help at all. Because panic is exactly what I did when my period didn't come last month. I was scared to death. I didn't know what to do. I needed someone to talk to and confide in, but I was too embarrassed to ask anybody anything! I mean everybody—my church friends, my school friends, my family—has me pegged as Miss Innocent.

It would have blown their minds if I had come to any one of them with my little crisis! But I had to do something.

When I saw a commercial on TV for an at-home pregnancy test kit, I decided that was my answer. Then at least I would know. If this were a false alarm, then no one would ever have to know what I had done. Except God. (I didn't even want to think about that!) I feel so deceitful on one hand. But in a way, I'm not that different from what everybody thinks. I'm not loose or promiscuous, and I accept what God says about sex outside of marriage. I just messed up, that's all.

It was mess-up enough to have gotten involved in the sexual encounter in the first place. But I certainly didn't think I would get pregnant. Now, I'm not stupid or naive. I realized, even at the time, that I was running the risk of getting pregnant. But I just didn't believe it would happen to me—not this one first time. I mean girls at school were forever talking about their little sexual escapades—how they hadn't really planned to get into anything, but "lost control."

It was an almost common lunchtime ritual to see some classmate, who was waiting eagerly for a menstrual period that was in definite jeopardy, march into the cafeteria and give the victory sign. Everyone who was privy to her plight, even guys, would laugh and whistle and applaud. Even though some of these girls were close personal friends, I don't think I was seduced by their so-called sexual freedom to want it for myself. In fact, even though I would laugh and cheer with everyone else when someone gave the victory sign, I saw nothing funny or enviable about these flirtations with pregnancy.

But I wonder now if I didn't become too familiar and too at ease with lifestyles and attitudes that needed to remain alarming and dangerous to me. I mean I've learned from experience that even though I want to be God-pleasing with my body, the hard, cold fact is, that in the face of serious temptation, it is not fear or love of God that keeps me in check, at least not directly! It is a healthy fear of getting pregnant.

Perhaps too many victory signs had dulled that healthy sense of fear and my resistance to temptation.

I usually didn't have to worry very much about temptation and resistance with my boyfriend, Jeffrey. We had agreed on the ground rules a long time ago. We drew the line at hugging (not the body-grinding kind!) and kissing (not the deep-throat ones that last from one date to the next!). And, of course, Momma imposed her own rules: where I could go, how long I could stay, who had to be there. Her restrictions weren't all that harsh, but they certainly guaranteed that we didn't get to spend much time alone together. Jeff and I had been going together for a year now, so he was used to it. Besides, we had known each other since junior high; he knew my mother was rather strict. In fact, I think he liked that. He used to spend almost as much time at our house as he did at his own—when my mother was home, of course. He was an only child, too, who lived with his father (his mother left them when he was six, but Jeff didn't like to talk about it). He always seemed shocked that even though there were just two of us, my mother and I still had family life and fun together.

Jeff graduated from high school three years ago and joined the army. But after a year, he was discharged because of a hearing defect. He came back home and got a job at the steel plant. Momma liked Jeff well enough. But even without her saying it directly, I could tell she was uneasy about the commitment developing between us. Whenever she heard me refer to Jeff as my boyfriend, she would interrupt and say something like this: "You just barely have permission to date. We don't have boyfriends yet, hear?" That's the way Momma is. She doesn't make something into a big issue most of the time, but she still makes her point.

But it didn't matter about the dating thing. It was just a matter of semantics to me. Technically, Momma was right. I only started going on real dates after I turned 16. (Most of my friends—even my cousins!—were allowed to date much earlier, but Momma had her own philosophy. "I'm not judging by the crowd. I'm judging by your maturity," was her enraging way of putting it. Even my uncle, her own brother, went to bat for me and tried to get her to ease up a little on the dating thing, but there had been no convincing Momma.) Anyway, Jeff was the only guy I'd really dated one-on-one, and we thought of ourselves as boyfriend and girlfriend. So what difference did it make if I refrained from making the reference around her? I could handle that.

KESI

I keep looking at the faces of some of the other women in the waiting room. I wonder how many of them are in the same position as me. Sitting in a place like this with your teenaged daughter, you can't help but ask that pointless question: "Where did I go wrong?" Without warning, my mind calls up a five-year-old memory photo of me and my sister, Cile, at her kitchen table. She and Colby had had a serious argument, and Colby had stormed out. As was her habit when these blowups occurred between her and my brother-in-law, Cile called me over to get my view on the "issue of the moment." This time, the issue had been, of all things, birth-control pills.

Their daughter, Melanie, was about to turn 16, and Cile wanted to give her, as part of her birthday present, a "gift certificate" for a visit to the gynecologist for a prescription for birth-control pills.

When Cile discussed the idea with Colby, he hit the ceiling. He considered it giving parental sanction and encouragement to unchristian behavior. Cile saw it as simply equipping her child to be responsible no matter which sexual choices she made. Colby had forbidden her to do it; Cile had told him this was "women's business" and something she had to do.

That day in the kitchen, she reminded me that Adisa was only a few years younger than Melanie, and that I would have to face the same decision. "People are always talking about how hard it is for single parents. But that's one advantage you have over us. You don't have to have these blowout arguments with anybody over how to raise your kids! So have you ever considered what you're going to do about Adisa—and when?"

"Actually, no," I answered thoughtfully. "I guess I agree with Colby. I don't think I would consider giving her birth-control pills as an option. I've taught her what's right, and that's what I expect her to do!"

"For heaven's sake, Kesi. I'm not giving her the pill! It's just a prescription. So that *if* she decides she can't wait, she can at least not complicate the mistake with an unwanted pregnancy."

"I know, Cile, but I still think the unspoken message is 'I don't expect you to be able to do the right thing,' and I *do!*"

"Boy, you and Colby! Both of you are naive and too idealistic for your own good! Well, I'm not going to let Melanie pay the price for it."

Had I been naive to expect my daughter to reject what was popular and follow the Christian training we'd given her? I'd always tried to help her see glamor and distinction in going against the tide. But why hadn't I seen this thing coming? If I had realized she was beginning to wrestle with her sexuality, I could have talked to her more directly about it. Maybe I had been naive. I can imagine what Cile would say if she knew where I was right now. (There's nothing she likes better than the words *I told you so.*) I keep looking at the memory to see if I've changed. But even now, with everything that's happened, I still feel the same way. (For some reason, that makes me feel good!) Of course, based on what Adisa told me, a prescription for birth-control pills would have made little difference in her case.

ADISA

I thought the visit would be over once they gave you "the verdict." But we're supposed to wait to see the staff psychologist and the family counselor. Back in the waiting room, I flip through a magazine to get my mind off this catastrophe. But it insists on remembering every detail.

The night we got into trouble Jeff had called from work, as he often did, to see if he could come by on his way home. The normal rule is if my mother is not home, I can't have company. But on this particular night, it was snowing pretty hard. Momma was due any minute. In fact, she should have been home early, because she was on jury duty and the courts let out earlier than her job. The snow was probably delaying her progress home. I figured by the time Jeff drove the 20 or so miles from his job, Momma would be home. I had told him to come ahead.

When Jeff arrived nearly an hour later, Momma still hadn't gotten home, and I was a little concerned. She hadn't called either. I met Jeff at the door. "Hey, your mother's car isn't here. She's not home?" he asked from the other side of the threshold.

I had stood shivering in the doorway explaining what had happened and why I was concerned. We stood there in a moment of indecision about what to do. I don't think either of us had any malicious intentions. I, for one, just wanted to finish our conversation without freezing to death. But the rule was standing there barring the entrance. I had taken the plunge.

"Come in a minute."

"Are you sure? I don't want to get you into any trouble," Jeff said, still from the safety of the other side of the doorsill.

"No, it's all right. Just stay for a moment and help me decide what to do."

Jeff had come in and joined me in the kitchen, the normal family gathering place. He was still in his coat, leaning against the wall. "She's probably on a case that ran overtime, that's all. I don't think it's anything to worry about. If anything had happened, she would have called. But you can't do that if you're in one of those jury rooms. I think they only let you make a phone call if you have to stay overnight."

I had mulled over his explanation. "You're probably right, but I'm going to watch the news just in case." I switched on the kitchen set.

Jeff had moved from the wall and plopped in a chair. His uneasiness about the broken house rule had obviously dissipated. Jeff peeled off his coat and tossed it over the back of his seat. "What do you have good to eat?"

I had rounded up a respectable provision of junk food and joined Jeff at the TV. The news reported no local catastrophes. Soon we had become light-spirited and engrossed in the game show that followed the news broadcast. During a commercial, Jeff had leaned over and kissed me gently, and I was totally submissive to the gesture. There had been something especially exciting about the moment. True enough it was forbidden, but it was also protected. We could take advantage of this special opportunity to be alone, because we had the built-in limitation of knowing my mother would be coming in the door any minute. The kissing became a little more arduous than usual.

The phone call had finally come. Momma explained hurriedly that her jury had been unexpectedly sequestered probably just for the night. She wanted me to pack a bag with a change of clothes and her toilet articles. Someone from the sheriff's office would come to pick it up. I was also to get whatever I needed to spend the night at my aunt's house. The deputy would drive me there. I was honestly going to tell her that Jeff was with me and could take me, but she was already issuing the last-minute warnings. "Make sure you see some identification when the deputy comes. Leave the kitchen light on. And put the deadbolt on the front door. Call Cile and tell her you're coming, 'cause I can only make this one call. But I know she's home. If you run into any problems that you can't handle, call your grandmother. Now, is everything all right? I'm sorry to rush you, but they're monitoring the calls to make sure we don't discuss the case and they've got 5 phones for 14 people! I hear it's snowing. Are you all right?"

Despite the fact that a mild sense of apprehension had resurfaced in me, I'd assured her that everything was fine. She had ended the conversation with her usual "Love you."

"I love you too, Ma," I'd said.

The minute I put down the phone, Jeff had grabbed me, held me flush against his body and kissed me. (It wasn't one of our normal hugs.) "And I love you too, Disa." He loosened his embrace a little to stare at me. "Did I hear what I think I heard? We get an evening," he wavered his eyebrows in a mockingly menacing fashion, "all alone?" I had pulled myself away from him, laughing, perhaps a little nervously.

"No, Knucklehead. I've got to pack a bag for Momma and

a bag for me. A deputy sheriff is coming for her clothes and to take me to Aunt Cile's. So you'd better get out of here so I can pack."

"No. I'll feel better if I stay until that deputy gets here. Who knows how long that might be."

Actually it hadn't been nearly long enough. The deputy must have been en route before my mother even hung up the phone! I had barely zipped up her overnight bag when he arrived; I hadn't made any progress on packing my own things. I had hurried to the door. Jeff, curious about the whole procedure, was at my side. "Ms. Graham?" The deputy had briefly flashed a badge. "I'm Officer Holloway. I'm to pick up a bag for Mrs. Kesi Graham and transport you to an address on Boarman Road. Are you all set?"

I had handed him Momma's bag and asked him if he could wait a few more minutes for me to finish getting ready. The officer looked at his watch. "Ma'am, I can't wait for you. We've got to get these people their things and I've got other pickups to make." He hesitated thoughtfully for a moment. "Now we are responsible for transporting you, so I tell you what. We'll dispatch another deputy for you later. But I'm afraid I can't say how soon or long before he'll be here. Will that be all right?"

"Disa, don't sweat it. I'll take you." Jeff had offered. But I was still looking at Officer Holloway, trying to decide how to answer him. I had been keenly aware that Jeff and I were on dangerous ground. We still had the lure and fascination of the forbidden, without any safeguards. I had been tempted but frightened by the prospect. The deputy, of course, could not perceive the critical substance of my thoughts. All he had seen was my quiet blank stare, and he responded accordingly.

"All right, Ms. Graham. Your mother should be back in circulation by tomorrow. If not, they'll be able to notify you in plenty of time. Y'all have a good evening." And he was gone.

I suppose from the unfair vantage point of hindsight, I would say that the inevitable happened. All evening long, with one detail after another, we had set ourselves up for failure. I can honestly say that I did not want to have sex with Jeff that night. And I certainly didn't "lose control." I had been willing to try to make this stolen moment of ours a little special. I had considered it a gift, an offering when I went beyond our normal rules to the limits of my own conscience. But when I said we had to stop, Jeff acted like someone who had been betrayed, wounded, and left to die. ("Baby, don't stop *now.* Please don't leave me hanging like this. Disa, please! I'm a man! What do you expect me to do?")

I had suddenly been faced with a mystery I didn't quite understand. He was earnestly pleading with me, as if for some critical act of mercy. And I was trying to think. This was far from the romantic vision I'd always had of my "first time"; there was no view, no sheer lace negligee, no candlelight, no music. I liked Jeff, maybe even loved him. But, I had suddenly realized, I never thought of him in terms of "forever." And suppose I got pregnant? But Jeff had been huddled beside me, moaning and pleading. I remembered the long parade of victory signs. (I knew this wasn't forever, but perhaps under the circumstances I should risk taking a chance.) I had let Jeff do what he needed to do. And he kept thanking me and telling me that he loved me.

KESI

I wish now that we had gone to my regular doctor. It was only embarrassment—sinful pride—that dissuaded me. It seems that everything I've heard about these clinics is true— an enormous patient load, small staff, and interminable waits. The waiting is the most aggravating. I can't seem to stop myself from spending these useless moments panning through every detail of what has happened, wondering what I might have done differently.

Even then, I could tell something was wrong.

Adisa is normally pretty even-tempered and not in the least reclusive. In fact, she usually met me at the door with some "lowdown" or another—something that was going on at school, or with someone in the family, or with her and Jeff. But during the past few weeks, I would come home and find her in her room. When I asked her why she was being so antisocial, she had apologized and said she was studying for some heavy midterms. Half the time, when I called her to dinner, she would say she wasn't hungry or didn't feel good.

I was starting to get concerned about her health and said something about making a doctor's appointment for her. That's when she finally told me she and Jeff had broken up. I remember reprimanding myself for not having recognized all the classic symptoms of a broken heart. I tried to get Disa to talk about it, and I was a little hurt and surprised that she didn't want to. But, I figured, this was her first heartbreak. She was still feeling her way on how to handle it. She knew I was there for her, so I decided not to press the issue. I was sorry to see her so unhappy, but I was privately relieved. I thought Jeffrey was a decent boy, but I just didn't see their lives heading in the same direction.

I was trying to be as tolerant as I could of Disa's low spirits, even when it resulted in uncharacteristic neglect of her household chores. (After all, how long could this moody slump of hers last?) So on the morning that she left for school without putting out the trash, I put aside my annoyance and decided to do it myself.

I was irked by the brown paper bag that clung to the plastic liner when I emptied the wastebasket in the bathroom. I snatched viciously at the offending bag, thinking it was empty. But the brown paper tore off in my hand, exposing an empty box. Emptying trash is such a mindless chore that I had already thrown the box in my sack of garbage before I realized what I had seen. I opened the garbage bag and stared at the pregnancy testing kit. I just kept looking at it, as if the writing on the package could explain what it was doing in my house! The clamor of the trash truck making its way down the alley roused me from my trance. I retrieved the package from the bag, put it in my purse, and finished putting out the trash. Then I hurried to work so my day could seem normal.

All day long I thought about "the box," trying to conceive of some explanation (other than the obvious) for why it was in our trash can. But it was hard to ignore the supportive evidence of Adisa's recent change of behavior. I felt an urgent need to talk to Adisa and find out what was happening in her life. But there was a part of me that was afraid—afraid of what I might discover and afraid of the confrontation and emotional pain (for both of us) it would take to find out.

That evening, at home, was quiet. I was almost grateful that Adisa didn't want dinner. I doubt if I could have sat through a meal together, keeping back all that was on my mind. Besides, I was enjoying this peaceful opportunity to meditate on what to do about my discovery. And I was depending on God to show me somehow.

Early the next morning, I had gone to Adisa's room and shaken her gently, waiting until I was certain she was fully awake.

"Adisa, what was the test result?" I asked quietly. "Are you pregnant?"

She hadn't even seemed surprised. She sat up, clawing nervously at the sheets. "I think so," she whispered huskily. "I'm not sure I did the test properly. I made an appointment at the clinic to be sure."

"Why, Adisa? Why?" I hadn't meant to sound anguished.

Then, in the midst of convulsive sobbing, she told me the story. I resisted the compassionate urge to cradle her in my arms, this child of mine who was, all of sudden, presenting herself to be a woman. "What do you plan to do? Had you planned to tell me at all?"

For the first time, she looked up at me, still crying. "I don't know, Momma. I don't know what to do. I can't think!"

She sank back down in the bed and pulled the sheets around her heaving shoulders. I watched the tears still streaming from beneath her closed eyelids. I should have comforted her. I should have offered her my forgiveness. Instead, I announced that I'd be going with her to the clinic, and I left the room.

ADISA

There is an eye-catching poster on the waiting room wall with a huge caption saying, "DON'T BE A STUD; BE A FATHER.

WE CAN HELP." Of course, I thought of Jeff. I haven't told him. Until today, it really didn't seem necessary. It's funny. (I keep seeing all these ironies!) When I so badly needed someone to talk to, I didn't turn to Jeff! I had had sex with the man, but somehow the matter of my missing period seemed too personal to discuss with him. In fact, our whole relationship became very awkward after that night. For the first couple of days, our sole concern had been whether Momma would find out that we had been alone together and start interrogating. (Had that deputy told her that he didn't have to drive me because "some guy" was there? Had Aunt Cile mentioned that Jeff had brought me to her house or how late it had been?)

When Momma came home that next day, she had been full of stories about her first experience as a juror—and being sequestered! Of course, she had asked, first thing, how I had made out. I had told her summarily that everything worked out fine. (I didn't lie about anything specific. I just didn't go into any details. In the midst of this major deceit, that seemed like the least of the evils.) And I baited her to tell me more about her jury deliberations (anything to get off the subject of that night!). I still couldn't be certain that the subject wouldn't come up when she had one of her almost daily conversations with Cile. But after three days passed with no evidence to indict me, I had been relieved enough to be able to refocus my anxiety on what had happened between Jeff and me.

He had called each day for an update on the success of our subterfuge and to see if it were okay for him to come by. I could tell he was nervous and worried about how I had been handling this new dimension in our relationship. I had assured him that we hadn't been found out, but each time I made excuses to discourage him from visiting. I hadn't wanted to see him. I was angry with him! (It took me awhile to realize that.) I knew I didn't have the right to be angry. (I mean, what we'd done was as much my fault as his.) But I was angry. And I didn't know how to let it out, and I wasn't sure I could keep it in.

I had been spending all my spare time in my room, trying

to figure out what was wrong with me. It wasn't the anger. It wasn't even the guilt. It was the paralyzing sense of helplessness that was depressing me! Something inside was urging me to pray. And I knew it would help me. But God, prayer, church, the kids in my Sunday school class—all those things that had for so long been a routine part of my life suddenly seemed distant and unfamiliar. I wasn't afraid to face God—I think I was too ashamed.

I had been cloistered in my room the day I heard Jeff's voice downstairs. It was unusual for him to come without calling first. In her innocence, Momma, with characteristic hospitality, had welcomed him to stay for dinner. I had hurried downstairs. "Jeff, what are you doing here?" Momma had looked at me rather oddly as she disappeared into the kitchen, leaving us alone in the living room. (Had my voice sounded accusing? too reprimanding?)

"I was dropping off some videos at a friend's house. I thought I'd take a chance and roll by. You busy?"

I would have set myself up for one of Momma's relentless interrogations if I had acted like I was anything other than delighted that Jeff was here. I had pointed him to a seat and sat down opposite him. Momma had the television on in the kitchen, so we had a safe measure of privacy.

"Are you okay, Disa? I've been a little worried about you."

"Yeah," I had done my best to sound casual. "I told you everything went okay."

"Are you upset with me about . . . about what happened?" Jeff had looked me squarely in the eye, but I had not been able to return his stare with the same candor.

"Let's just say I'm a little upset with both of us, okay? It shouldn't have happened, but it did. So that's that." I heard the edge in my own voice. Jeff was quiet for a minute; I knew he had heard the pique in my tone.

"You're right, it shouldn't have happened. And I'm truly sorry that it wasn't the way I would have had it be for us."

Oblivious to the whole drama, Momma had interrupted us: "Jeff, I'm setting the table. You going to stay?"

Jeff had looked at me for endorsement, but I stared into

my lap. "No, Mrs. Graham. I can't today. Thanks for the invitation."

I could tell that Jeff had been hurt and probably more than a little mystified by my retreat from him. I felt sorry for him and frustrated that I hadn't been able to be more honest with him. I walked him to his car where he made one last attempt to get through to me. "Adisa, please don't think I'm taking what we did lightly. You're very special to me. I've been doing a lot of thinking over the past few days. Listen, we need to talk. When can we get together?"

"I want to talk too, Jeff. Just give me a couple of days to get my thoughts together. Okay?" I had kissed him on the cheek, both to encourage him to accept my offer without objection and to forestall any more intimate farewell gesture. Jeff had nodded complacently and left.

KESI

They call Adisa's number, and we are directed to the psychologist's office. But as it turns out, she wants to talk to us separately. She seats me in a comfortable outer office where I am, thankfully, alone—but, once again, waiting and thinking.

At first I couldn't understand what happened to me that morning when Adisa finally told me her story. My child poured out her heart to me, and I left her crying in her bed! (I have no doubt that that scene is now in my memory album.)

But when I went back to my own bed that same morning, another memory photo came instantly to mind that deciphered the mystery of my own behavior. It is not a memory I had forgotten, but one I had painstakingly suppressed. The memory photo is of me, lying in my bed. There is a man beside me in the bed, but he is not in the picture. It is a close-up of my face with an empty, almost expressionless stare. It was about five years after Evan died. I was a reasonably happy woman. I had a social life, but I'd never really gotten into dating. For a long time, I hadn't wanted to. (Evan still seemed such a part of me.) But later it just seemed inconvenient. Apart from being busy with a career and parenting, I worried about the impact of dating on my role as a mother. I'd had friends, widows and divorcees, who had run into serious conflicts when their children felt threatened by new relationships. I had been afraid to take that risk with Adisa. But there had been that one time. The details, not even the person, were part of the memory photo. It was just that the entire time Adisa was telling me "it had just been this one time," "she hadn't meant for it to happen," and how guilty she'd felt, she was narrating the story of that suppressed memory of mine.

There I was, righteously abhorrent of the sinful failure of my 18-year-old daughter, and I, as a grown, spiritually mature woman, had made the same mistake. I had run from that painful truth in her bedroom that morning, but I had wrestled with it every day since. I long ago asked God's forgiveness for my own sexual sin, but my behavior with Adisa that morning made me question whether I had accepted it.

ADISA

When I first made this appointment, I had expected to come alone—to just be a "big girl" and deal with whatever I had to. In fact, at certain points, I was very self-conscious and uncomfortable about Momma being with me. But now, facing this psychologist by myself, I feel like a scared little kid. She wants to know if there is anything I want to talk over or any problems and stresses I might need help with. But, of course, my mind goes totally blank. I keep staring at her, not saying a word!

"Take your time," she says soothingly. "I'm going to step outside and talk with your mom, and then I'll be back to see if there's anything we need to talk over."

As I watched her go, I thought of how desperately I'd needed someone to talk to a couple of weeks ago. I wouldn't have hesitated to talk to an even half-interested stranger then, but right now I was a little hesitant about the prospect. There was certainly plenty to talk about, especially the situation with Jeff. I did eventually call him and agreed to go out to a movie.

Of course, we both had known what this date was really about. But I think each of us had welcomed the diversion of the movie to help dilute the tension.

Afterward, at the pancake house, I stared into my mug of hot apple cider as I told him the truth about how I felt. I liked him. We were friends. But the sexual encounter had been inappropriate. We shouldn't glamorize what we had done or try to make our relationship more than what it was because of what we'd done. I hoped that we hadn't damaged our friendship by bringing sex into it, but we may have. It would take time for me to put that part behind me.

I had put a lot of time and thought into that speech, especially trying to make it friendly and tactful. I had been careful to edit out any anger. So I was totally unprepared for Jeff's reaction to it. He had seethed!

"If you didn't want to make love with me, then why did you?" His teeth were clenched and his eyes were glaring as he spat out each word with slow deliberation. I had stared at him in disbelief. My mind was playing back this video of him moaning and begging and my being rattled by it. My eyes had misted over, and I hadn't been able to answer him.

"Can we go, please?" I asked instead. We rode home that night in silent and mutual anger. When I got out of the car, Jeff said, "I don't know what's going on here. So I guess it's up to you."

I had lain in bed that night thinking. And I realized that Jeff had told the truth. He really didn't know what was going on. And I was only beginning to understand how immature and unready we had been. That night I had gone to sleep with a peaceful sense of resolution. I wasn't angry anymore. I had learned an expensive lesson, and I was going to put the whole unfortunate incident behind me. But only today am I discovering that that lesson is going to cost me in ways I had never envisioned. I hadn't really planned on seeing Jeff again. Now I'm not sure what I'm going to do. I was still absorbed in that thought when the psychologist came back into the office.

"Adisa?" she calls me to attention. "Did you think of anything?"

I decide that she is not the one I want to talk to. "No, I think I'll be okay."

"Fine!" she says, smiling at me. "Then we'll have your mom come in, and the family counselor will be with you both in a moment."

She disappears, and Momma comes in. My back is to her, but I can feel her looking at me. I am mildly curious about what she may have confided to the psychologist. And, knowing Momma, I suspect she would want to know what I said. (Wouldn't she be surprised!) But neither of us seems to be able to come up with anything to take the edge off the stressful silence.

Mercifully, the counselor comes in. She is just what this moment needs. She is a short, grandmotherly woman who makes up for her unimposing appearance with an infectiously lively personality. She hovers for a moment in the doorway, openly staring at us. "Hi. I'm Lottie. Let me guess—mother and daughter, right? I'd recognize this misery anywhere!" she adds with a chuckle.

I can't help myself. I laugh at the thought of what Momma and I must have looked like, trying to avoid each other in this tiny room. "Ladies, let me give you a little piece of advice. Relax and get used to being uncomfortable. If you're fortunate, you'll be talking together about a lot of touchy subjects over the next few weeks. So let's get past the impasse right now. Stand up, sweetheart." Lottie is talking to me in her grandmotherly tone that seems to work. I stand up hesitantly. She places her arm around my shoulder and turns me around to face my mother. "Now look at each other." In a quick clandestine glance, I see that Momma is staring vaguely in my direction. I drop my eyes reflexively.

"No, look at each other." Lottie coddles my chin up from its perch on my chest while she corrects Momma with her voice and eyes. We are looking at each other now with neutral stares. "Do you love your daughter, Mother?"

I am surprised by the brazen emphatic tone of Momma's answer. "Yes," she says, maintaining, with obvious effort, a stranglehold on my gaze.

"Daughter, do you love your mother?" Lottie continues.

"Yes," I reciprocate with relief.

"Good!" Lottie applauds. "That's all I needed to know. And I think you two needed reminding. Now let's talk about some of those touchy subjects."

She has Momma sit down in her chair. She explains tactfully from her perch on the desktop that some clients opt not to become mothers, and the clinic does offer alternatives. She outlines the clinic's abortion procedures and adoption program and suggests we talk about them as soon as possible. "Well, that's my whole spiel!" Lottie says, packing up her papers. She stops in the doorway and looks at us with pleading eyes. "Don't forget. You love each other. Don't lose sight of that." She monitors us with her gaze for a few moments and goes.

Neither Momma nor I speak a word as we leave the clinic. We have a long walk to the parking garage. This time, the silence between us is comfortable, absorbing, and busy. The clinic visit had done me a world of good, especially Lottie's contribution. She was tender and loving and, for the first time, my heavy spirit was eased. I feel a little more ready to face the issues I was avoiding.

KESI

The sunshine feels like a welcome embrace as we leave the clinic. I look back over my shoulder at the lesson its plain, unimpressive facade presented me: God has His angels everywhere! I don't know the first thing about Lottie, not even her last name! But she had brought healing through the simple but powerful exchange she orchestrated between Adisa and me.

I look over at her. I am pleased to notice she is not wearing the sullen scowl she has been using to protect herself. I am anxious to take advantage of the miracle's magic and talk. But Adisa seems so absorbed in her own thoughts. I decide not to intrude yet.

I am looking at the faces of the other pedestrians we pass on our pilgrimage to the car, but it is still Adisa's face that I see. I wonder what it will be like for her—being a single mother. Maybe it will not be as difficult for her as it was for me, because she won't have all the years of having a partner to compare it to. But neither will she experience the miracle of seeing two lives being seasoned and cultivated into a comfortable oneness—the planning together and working together, the give-and-take. I think again of Cile, and I can't help smiling at the irony. She is rankled by having to argue with Colby over parenting decisions, and I get nervous about making those decisions without that other parent to thrash it over with. But, of course, my family and a few trusted friends have always been there to fill the void. That thought brings another smile. There had been so many times when that support group, especially my family, not only wanted to fill the void, they wanted to take over completely! (We had some scenes all right!) But I could also remember some crises that had so overwhelmed me that I was almost willing to let them.

I looked over at Adisa again. I would have to keep remembering those times and restrain myself from taking over her new responsibility.

Responsibility. For some reason, the word makes me think of finances, an unwelcome intrusion in my reverie. There will be medical expenses. (I think my health insurance will cover most of it, but I need to check.) But what about afterwards? The cost of another life—formula, diapers, clothes, a pediatrician—could easily decimate our 20-years' savings. Low-grade anxiety begins to rise in me, complicated by mild pangs of guilt about taking my secure and comfortable lifestyle for granted. (I can't remember when I last thanked God just for His ample day-to-day provision!) I calm myself by thinking of Lottie, my own little reminder of 'God's rescue and forgiveness. Besides, I may be jumping the gun entirely in assuming I will be taking care of Adisa and the baby by myself. I have written Jeff out of the picture completely! I suddenly realize how little I really know about this character. He is not my ideal vision of a son-in-law. (Who is?) And Adisa says they have broken up. (Whatever that means!) But now, with the baby, maybe they'll ... I don't even bother to finish the thought. It sounds too old-fashioned, even to me!

KESI and ADISA

"Momma?" Adisa broke the silence first, "can we talk?" We have finally reached the car and are comfortably alone together inside. She didn't have to wait for my answer.

"I've been doing some serious thinking. I don't think I want to have a baby. This whole thing has been a mistake. Jeff isn't the guy for me. I want to go to college and have a career."

"Adisa, having a baby doesn't mean you can't go to college and have a career. It may take a little longer and be more difficult for you, but ..."

"Momma," she interrupts me gently, "I want to have an abortion." She races ahead, anticipating my objection. "I know it isn't right. But neither is any of the rest of it."

I refuse to get upset. Watch what you say, I coach myself. Don't turn her off.

"What about adoption, Disa?" I ask in an even tone.

"I thought about it. But once I have a baby, it would be mine. I couldn't stand the thought of someone else raising my baby! I'd never stop wondering if it was being cared for and happy."

"Adisa, it already *is* your baby!" I caress her stomach gently. "It's not out here in the world yet, but it's already yours to wonder about and care for." She is quiet. And then I say something I had not expected to say. But as I speak, I realize how much I mean it. "Adisa, I had planned to leave this decision up to you. I felt I could live with either choice you made. I don't want to see you have to take on the responsibility of being a mother right now. And I'm not looking forward to what it will mean for me either. So I have plenty of motive to succumb to the temptation of abortion. But I can't watch you add to the guilt you're smothering yourself in. Adisa, have you asked God to forgive you?"

She begins to cry quietly, shaking her head. This time I do cradle her in my arms. She sobs into my shoulder, "I can't. I knew it was wrong, and I did it anyway."

I push her away from me so I can look at her face. For a moment, I consider telling her my own story, but I decide the moral is more important than the tale. "Adisa, that's what forgiveness is for! You're thinking big sins and little sins. Forgiveness is for all of them. Did you think you were too good to be guilty of this one?"

She didn't have to answer. I hug her against me tightly. "You're not, honey. None of us is."

During a thoughtful hush, the sobbing downgrades to sniffles, and Adisa gradually pulls herself out of my embrace. She is staring at the windshield, not arrogant, but resolute. "Momma, I'm not saying that I'm going to go against you. But it has to be my decision. Lottie said the clinic doesn't require parental consent for 18-year-olds. As she finishes her statement, she faces me meekly, as if to soften the blow of her words.

The miracle's magic is still working. I am not angry or threatened by her honesty. "Disa, I'm not concerned about whether the clinic respects my consent. I'm concerned whether my daughter does."

"What would you do if I decided to have an abortion?" I can tell she is genuinely curious. And I respond honestly.

"I don't know. I'd have to deal with having a daughter who refuses to respect my authority." I can sense her bristling at my pulling rank. "I can only say two things I'm certain I'd do: I wouldn't stop praying until I knew the right thing to do. And I wouldn't stop loving you." I am surprised to realize that I am smiling at her. I guess I'm vaguely sure she won't compound her problems with an abortion.

But Adisa is staring at the windshield again. "Are you going to tell everybody I'm pregnant?"

I am speaking with peculiar confidence now. "I'm not going to send out a press release, if that's what you mean. But I'm not going to keep it a secret. Sometimes other people can profit from our mistakes." (I am thinking of all the memory photos I have seen today.)

"Suppose you tell everyone I'm pregnant, and I end up having an abortion?"

"Then I guess that'll be one more mistake to learn from," I answer quietly.

There is another lull. This time I break the silence. "What about Jeff? Have you considered what he's going to say?"

She shakes her head, still staring blindly through the glass. "I haven't told him. And I'm not sure what he thinks is going to matter to me. He's not the one whose life will change." There is a bitter edge to her tone.

"Don't write him off like that, Disa." She looks at me abruptly, more than a little surprised by my attitude. "You know, your dad always used to say that even when a man and a woman break up, they should leave each other healing instead of hating."

There is a sudden stir of activity in the garage and the sounds of a work day coming to an end. (I had lost all awareness of the time.) I reach out to start the car, but Adisa stops my hand with hers. "Momma, I'm sorry about everything."

"I know, honey." And I add in a raspy whisper, "I love you." I hug her again, hiding my tears in her hair, hoping she'll remember.

An Encouraging Word

Kesi discovers her 18-year-old single daughter is pregnant, and she feels nothing. Her first response is numbness—a natural reaction as well as a necessary safety feature built into her inmost being. Numbness manifests a shock reaction—Adisa's announcement is almost more than Kesi can bear. And what dedicated mother would not feel the same, anticipating and wanting the best for her offspring and seeing those dreams crumble before her very eyes?

Kesi has wanted not only the best for Adisa, but better than she had had in her own youth. She has identified education as the road to achieving the equality and sense of self-worth she herself had missed until her late college years. Would Adisa's education now be terminated? Would the advent of her child switch her, possibly for the rest of her life, from life's forward track to a dead end? How threatening a thought to this mother!

It is interesting to note that the intended message of Kesi's name—"the trouble black people were in"—now describes her own daughter, not because she is black, but because she is pregnant. This crisis situation threatens and mocks the central commitment Kesi and her husband had shared. Even the reason they chose the name *Adisa* for their daughter, hoping she would communicate a liberated mindset to peers, was being negated. Instead, her daughter adopted the sexual expressions of her teenage group. Adisa's situation strikes a familiar chord from Kesi's past, magnifying Kesi's reaction and intensifying the feelings she has. Would Kesi be able to cope and cope effectively? What a challenge!

The "If Onlys"

Kesi's reaction follows a course all too familiar to many women. From barren numbness she steps ankle deep into self-recrimination. "If only I could have been home, this would not have happened." "If only I had not been required to stay overnight for the court matter." Although it is most profitable to explore and learn from our behavior, including our mistakes, "if onlys" amount to nothing other than unnecessary self-torture. We gain nothing by voicing or thinking them, and we lose much. Self-punishment clouds our forward thinking.

Adisa, on the other hand, has been operating on the denial and rationalization typical of first sexual encounters. "A pregnancy won't happen to me," she tells herself. Strangely enough, denial and rationalization don't end after one or several one-night stands. Repeated encounters frequently reinforce the unreality that surrounds the eating of forbidden fruit. Most likely, Adisa's teenaged friends operated on this premise as well.

In the discussion between Cile and Colby, Kesi's sister and brother-in-law, regarding birth-control pills, we witness their opportunity to air different perspectives constructively. Unfortunately, each parent promotes adoption of a unilateral position—his or her own. Nothing seems to be accomplished except by authoritarian dictate. Father says, "You may not"; Mother says, "I shall and I will." Being stuck in that power struggle closes off the opportunity to look beyond themselves, to pursue the issue more openly, to look for other guidance.

"The Grass Is Greener"

Furthermore, it is interesting to note how Cile and Kesi, coming from different parenting perspectives, see the other as having an advantage. Cile believes having no spouse has to be better than being married to one who argues with her. Kesi sees no spouse as missing a childrearing partner. This may well reflect, in a broader sense, that all-too-human trait of ours that believes "the grass is greener on the other side."

It also demonstrates the difficulty we have focusing on our own God-given advantages. Not only do we often fail to appreciate them, but as a result we probably won't explore them to the fullest. We frequently suffer from "material myopia" and view our situation in a nearsighted fashion, instead of a more global Christian perspective. Our Lord never gives us more than we can deal with. All things work together for good to those who love God. How difficult it is to accept His plan. How omnipotent a position we frequently take in thinking we can devise better outcomes than God can.

Can Kesi recall that during her own pregnancy, in being part of God's process of creation, she was brought closer to God? Might not the same thing apply to Adisa?

A Contrast in Parenting

Kesi and Cile present a sharp contrast in approaches to parenting. So do Adisa and her boyfriend, Jeff. Unaccustomed to family life, Jeff also was the product of a single-parent household. His mother left when he was six. If he experienced little or no family life, and never even had fun times with a parent, who taught him his values? Who taught him Christian standards? With no modeling at home, who taught him sensitivity to another's feelings, particularly a female's?

The way Kesi raised Adisa presents an opposite example of parenting. She thrust all her efforts into a career and parenting, without much of a life of her own. Little could she realize that this might lead to expecting more of her child in return. Kesi may not have allowed herself to be forgiven by accepting God's forgiveness for one of her own mistakes, so it is understandable she would project onto Adisa difficulty believing in God's grace and mercy. This is demonstrated when Adisa confides in her mother about the pregnancy, and Kesi resists the urge to cradle her daughter in her arms. Rather she pulls away, detaching herself. Her shock, hurt, and anger come through without Kesi's even realizing it.

Anger, a Telltale Indicator

If we are willing, we can use our own tendencies toward detachment and aloofness as indicators of our own anger: anger with ourselves as well as with another. The same applies to hurt, which often is camouflaged and comes out as anger.

It is both impressive and commendable that this devastated mother made attempts to understand her own detachment.

Adisa's emotions center first around denial, then anger at herself and Jeff, along with heavy guilt, helplessness, and depression. She responds by withdrawing. After all, she is floundering in an abyss of confusion and uncertainty. To whom can she turn? She does not even turn to the Savior through prayer, regarding herself as being undeserving. She retreats into herself, which only compounds the confusion. At last, her difficulty in reaching out to anyone notwithstanding, she thinks of making the clinic appointment. In doing so, she opens the door through which some help can enter.

In the clinic experience, Adisa, apparently uncomfortable, respects her own intuitive feelings when she decides not to confer with the psychologist. Here is a good point to underscore: if you don't feel comfortable with a particular therapist, that therapist is not right for you.

In contrast, the family counselor demonstrates warmth and empathy, and both Kesi and Adisa feel comfortable with her. She breaks down the wall between them and prompts what has been missing—awareness of love and caring, expressed verbally. She helps them break through their distancing stance. They do not lose sight of the love that exists between them. This time, the first session with a therapist worked well, probably because Kesi's and Adisa's distancing stance was not entrenched by years of hostility.

Alternatives

Following the clinic experience, Adisa and Kesi explore alternatives—a healthy approach. The temptation frequently is to take the short-term, easy way out, without looking at long-range considerations. No wonder Adisa first thought about abortion. Her guilt and shame kept her from asking for God's forgiveness, as if God reserves pardon for people who don't need it. Until we trust God to forgive our sins, we may not be open to forgiving ourselves.

Kesi's love for the Lord stimulates her to remind her daughter of God's forgiving power. In hugging Adisa and being sensitive to her daughter's feelings, she demonstrates her love

113

and acceptance of her, not qualifying it by judgmental expressions of her behavior. And how important it is for us to remember who provides this: God Himself is the author of love and acceptance.

The theme of profiting from mistakes surfaces once more. How healthy it is to take this attitude! Since we are all sinful and will therefore make mistakes, the very best we can do is to learn from them. We can recognize the power of God's forgiveness. We can be open to forgiving ourselves. We can learn new ways to avoid repeating our mistake. This is the attitude Kesi promotes. Here is Christian parenting at its best. This God-fearing mother's love for the Lord becomes apparent through her Christian parenting. She is not perfect and recognizes it.

Adisa's predicament is not a sign that Kesi has failed as a mother. Holding back from being critical and judgmental, she shows compassion and caring instead. She offers support and makes herself available to her daughter, without trying to placate or appease her. Nor does she accuse or attack Adisa, resisting the defensive urge to excuse herself. She does not attempt to smooth over but offers understanding.

Kesi's many inner strengths are readily demonstrated, and she appears to recognize the source of these gifts. She copes as effectively as she did because she relied on her faith. Adisa, in her youthfulness, stands on the same foundation. The love of both mother and daughter has been tested, and it not only survives, but thrives. The reader is left with the impression that they have been brought even closer together—as is often the case with crises. They will be even better prepared to handle the difficulties ahead of them.

A Parent's Struggles

Kesi provides an excellent example of the many struggles parents encounter, and especially of the unique challenges facing a single parent. In turn, Adisa provides an excellent example of the unique struggles encountered by a Christian teenager. Together their handling of these difficulties offers a powerful example of God's grace at work in their lives.

For Parental Exploration

This gripping but touching story stimulates exploration of a difficult area that lies before all parents. Where and to what degree should cautionary restrictions be imposed? What is too firm and what is too lenient? Where should lines be drawn? On the one hand, all youth want and need guidelines and restrictions (many of which are unwelcomed at the time). They need, as well, the teaching of Christian values.

However, if parents lay down restrictions that are too firm, they may unintentionally send a message that says their children are not capable or trustworthy. This provokes rebellion. On the other hand, if parents are too lenient, teenagers, in their own immaturity, may not be able to integrate values into their lives without assistance. Where to draw the line— a most difficult question!

How can parents effectively walk the line between too much and too little? Ongoing and consistent teaching and modeling of Christian values is a must. Open discussion and personal sharing frequently prove to be more helpful than gratuitous advice. A mother's honest and frank discussion about periods of temptation in her own life, and ways of handling it, will free a teenager to open up as well. Offer opportunities within limits for youth to practice their values and make their own decisions. The small-step, limited-dose approach can never be overemphasized.

Furthermore, routine family conferences are vitally important. Here everybody discusses a predicament (including the feelings that go with it), and the other family members respond and become involved by offering a variety of solutions. Consider eliciting imaginary circumstances and what one may do to handle them—a kind of dress rehearsal for problem solving and coping with temptation.

Finally, learn about your child's developmental level. This helps parents know what they can expect from their children. Frequently discuss what children may readily encounter at their age level, their feelings regarding it, and alternative ways of handling the situation.

Our Journeys, Our Lives
Our lives are journeys—to growth and wholeness: growth of a child, growth of a parent, and growth of relationships. What is this growth? In the final analysis, growth is the process of moving from compulsion toward choice, from fear toward confidence, and from withdrawal toward closeness.

Doris R. McElwee

Reflection

- Which character in the story seems most like you? List the similarities.

- At the end of their story how did Kesi see herself? How did Adisa see herself? In what specific ways did you see God's grace at work in their lives?

- Have you experienced God's undeserved love? How has this affected the way you feel about yourself? about others? What reassurance could you share with a struggling single parent?

- Kesi's sister (Cile) believes that single parents have the advantage of not having to argue with spouses over parenting decisions. Do you agree with Cile? Can you think of any advantages of single parenting?

- What unique struggles do you see in the lives of single parents? Can you think of any ways in which single parents can counteract the negative impacts of not having a child-rearing partner?

- Read and mediate on these accounts of God at work in the life of a single parent: 1 Kings 17; 2 Kings 4:1–7; Genesis 21:8–21; Luke 7:11–15. What encouragement do these accounts offer?

- Consider forming a support group for single parents in your congregation. Share Bible study, prayer, and fellowship.

A Final Word from Kesi and Adisa

Kesi

A favorite song of mine goes like this: "My soul looks back and wonders just how I got over . . ." I have every confidence that someday I'll sing it to celebrate this trial. But for now a passage from 2 Timothy sustains me. It soothes and excites me, especially when I hear it from the King James version, the way my grandmother always proclaimed it: "I am not ashamed: for I know whom I have believed, and am persuaded that he is able to keep that which I have committed unto him against that day" (2 Timothy 1:12 KJV).

Adisa

I guess it is true that troubles bring you closer to God. I used to read the Bible to get ready for Sunday school or when we were in church. But now I read it just for me. And I've discovered a passage in Psalm 91 that has become like Jesus' personal message to me. It gives me encouragement and energy every time I read it. I know it by heart now; and when I say it to myself, I make it my message: *"Because she loves me," says the Lord, "I will rescue her; I will protect her, for she acknowledges my name. She will call upon me and I will answer her; I will be with her in trouble, I will deliver her and honor her. With long life will I satisfy her and show her my salvation."*

Dear God,
When my life crumbles,
Sin stares back.
I have nowhere to run
Except to Your
Loving arms.

Your grace covers me,
Lifts me,
Reassures me,
Wraps me round,
Makes me strong.

When others stumble,
Put me there
To hold them tight,
Love them long,
Dry their tears . . . for You.

Amen.

Abby: From Mourning to Dancing

by Martha Streufert Jander

Abby

December 24, 11:20 p.m

Journaling—a new venture for me. My best friend, Colleen
Denison, gave me this journal for an early Christmas gift. She's
been after me for a long time to "journal," as she calls it. "It's
the thing that's kept me sane," she tells me as she shows me
her five or six volumes, each inscribed on the inside cover
with these cryptic words:

> *If I should die before I wake,*
> *Please throw my journals in the lake.*

Not a bad idea. I plan to keep my journals under lock and
key with a note to Lisa that they are not to be opened and
read until her grandchildren have grandchildren. They won't
know anything at all about Abigail Richards, except that she
was their three times great-grandmother.

It's Christmas Eve, and Gordon has taken the three children to the midnight service at church. I have been suffering
from a bad sinus infection the last few days and so begged
off accompanying them.

After they left, I wrapped a few last gifts, filled the stockings and hung them on the mantel, and now am sitting with
a cup of herbal tea between the glow of the smoldering em-
bers in the fireplace and the rainbow glow of the Christmas
tree.

While I sit here gazing at the tree—of course, the most
beautiful one we've had so far (isn't each one like that?)—I
am flooded with Christmas memories. I think back to my own
childhood—the joyful anticipation, the mounting excitement,

the mysterious packages under the tree, the Christmas service at church that always kept us in mind of the real reason for Christmas—the birthday of our Lord and Savior, Jesus Christ.

I was always determined that my children—whoops! scratch that *my*—Gordon always accuses me of doing that when I talk about the kids—*our* children should experience the same kind of joy and love at this holy time of the year. And up until the last few years, we've been able to do that.

Christmases when the children were young I remember with joy and pleasure. Gordon and I didn't have a lot of money to spend, but we had fun spending what we had budgeted. (I wonder what's turned him into such a scrooge this past year.)

We always sat up late, usually on Christmas Eve, putting together the toys we had bought, setting them under the tree, filling the little stockings with surprises.

Since Megan turned 14 last June—and she's our baby—I can't dream anymore of having baby dolls and trucks and tricycles under the tree. Now Lisa, at 20, wants things for college, 17-year-old Matt is into Nintendo games, and for Megan it's clothes.

Or, each one might say, "Oh, Mom, just give me money!" Don't they know how much pleasure I get out of choosing just the right thing for them? I guess not.

And then there's Gordon. He's gotten almost impossible to buy for. The last couple of years, actually since he turned 45 just two years ago, he isn't (can't be, won't be) pleased with anything I buy for him.

I can predict already that he'll be at the store two days from now exchanging the set of power tools I bought for him and the jacket as well. Now he is one I sometimes feel I could give money to and not feel bad about it at all.

Well, tomorrow is Christmas. We'll celebrate with Gordon's parents this year, since I finally talked my mother into visiting my younger sister Julie in Minnesota. And then Mom took the train. We couldn't for the world convince her that air traffic is safer—to say nothing of being much quicker. If only Dad were still alive—he was the one to look for adventures, and more often than not, Mom would go along with him. But since he died five years ago, she hasn't shown much interest in anything that goes on outside of her own little apartment at Woodson Lakes. I'm so glad she decided to move to this combination nursing home/retirement home for older people who don't want to be totally on their own. She's dropped out of everything but the evening guild at church.

Mom and Dad Richards will be coming here right after church, so we're delaying opening gifts until then. I'm glad those two still have each other.

Right now I feel the peace of Christmas—the joy of knowing Jesus as Savior—the Savior of the world and my Savior. I wish I could reach out to the whole world with that same peace and joy. I wish I could give Gordon some of that peace. Maybe he'll feel some of it tonight too. He seems to need it these days.

Better close for now. I heard the garage door opener whirr on. And I do need to find a safe place for this book.

January 6

It's Epiphany, and I'm just now making another entry into this book. I'm sitting in the living room again, this time with the Christmas tree lights on for the last time this season.

Gordon reminded me last night that the tree always comes down on January 6. I'm not sure why he always tells me that. Especially since—as usual—he is out of town and will not be around to help "undo" it.

As for me, I could keep the tree up until the end of January. But then, I don't seem to have a voice in the matter. So, down it will come to be packed away until next Christmas.

By the way, Gordon did exchange the set of power tools for an upgraded set, just as I thought he would. Surprisingly he kept the jacket. I will say he behaved decently on Christmas, though I could see the little muscles in his jaw work when he opened the power tools, as if I'm supposed to know what he really wants without his ever saying a word about it.

He didn't say anything at the time, but then what could

he say, I guess, with his parents there? I'm sorry. That wasn't very nice. But he seemed to be part of the family for most of that day at least. Except that he couldn't understand that if he said dinner would be at 2:00, why we weren't eating at 2:15 yet. (Not that he helped straighten things in the living room after gift giving or got his parents their eggnog. Well, at least it's over for another year.)

I must say I enjoy Mom and Dad Richards. We always seem to get along okay. But I did see his mother give Gordon some funny looks when they were here. I wish I could sit and talk to her about it, but how do you admit to your mother-in-law that her son doesn't seem to care about his wife anymore?

His gift to me sure indicated that—a gaudy three-piece suit I wouldn't be buried in, much less wear to work. Besides, it was too small—another of his hints, maybe, that I need to shed a few pounds?

His choice makes me wonder if he ever opens his eyes to look at the real me—what I really like and enjoy. I feel like I put so much thought and effort into his gifts, and he exchanges them, usually for a different model or one almost the same, but a little more expensive.

His gifts to me seem to be the first thing in the store he sees, no matter if they are unsuitable. Maybe next week I'll quietly exchange it for something I like. These days, I'm not sure Gordon would even notice.

In a way, I'm relieved Christmas is over. I like to shop and bake and get the house ready, but if Gordon's *schedule* is upset too much, *he* becomes upset. December would be an upsetting month anyway, even if I hadn't gone back to work a year ago. But Gordon shouldn't be so constantly upset; it was his idea.

I used to be able to keep things fairly neat and clean around the house. I got laundry and ironing done on schedule, even made breakfast so the five of us could eat together in the morning. But my working outside the home has thrown that all off course.

And I never hear the end of it—"I don't see why we can't eat every night at 6:30." "This room looks like a disaster area!

When are you going to clean it?" "This bank statement is messed up again! Abby, can't you do a little simple math?"

Nothing I do ever seems to satisfy him anymore. Even my appearance comes under attack more and more, as if I don't see the gray in my hair and the extra pounds around my hips. I think since I began working again full-time, our relationship has deteriorated.

We used to get along fairly well (according to Colleen, we had a terrific marriage) and even had time for fun occasionally. I don't know— maybe he's going through his second childhood or maybe it's midlife crisis. It certainly is his midlife, and it seems to me we are constantly in a state of crisis. Colleen had warned me—and that's why she gave me this journal.

January 9

My journaling on January 6 seems to be rather chaotic. I did ramble quite a bit, didn't I? I guess I was feeling a little down that day, because Lisa had just left that morning to go back to college. She always leaves a hole in the family. We don't seem to be quite complete when she's gone. Actually, that happens when any one of the children is away for any length of time.

Well, the tree is down and put into storage for another year. It wasn't as bad as I thought the other night. I had put some Christmas music on and was getting into a proper mood. Just as I was starting to wrap up the ornaments, Megan came home from basketball practice and helped me. She got rather nostalgic about Christmas (at the ripe old age of 14), so we laughed and talked together.

I guess that's one good thing about your kids growing up—they can become friends instead of just little ones to take care of.

While we were still visiting over hot chocolate and Christmas cookies, Matt arrived home from basketball practice and joined us. Since there were just the three of us, we ate a

127

rather late supper (yes, after the hot chocolate and cookies—
Gordon would have had a fit!).

I was glad Matt and Megan showed up when they did, for
if I had had to take down the tree with all the ornaments
they—and Lisa—had made when they were little, I would
have gotten very weepy.

January 11

After supper tonight I picked up Mom from the train sta-
tion. I just don't like that part of town, especially on dark,
wet, rainy nights like tonight. But I got her back to her little
place and all settled in. We did have to make a side trip to
the grocery store, however, to pick up some milk and bread—
just a few things (it's always just "a few things").

She seems to have had a good time at Julie's. She talked
a lot about Julie and Dan's two young ones. Johnny is seven
and Rachel is three. I wouldn't have minded going up there
myself to enjoy a Christmas with little ones again.

I'm glad Mom's trip turned out well. If it hadn't, I'm sure
I would be sitting here, blaming myself for talking her into
going. As it is, she mentioned that Julie and Dan want her to
come up north this summer for a month, and she just might
go. I'll have to keep that thought in mind and encourage her!

I feel pulled in so many directions. And Mom, so often,
doesn't seem to realize the other demands on my life—driving
the children places, working at the nursing home and at home
here. She thinks I can drop everything I'm doing to drive her
where she wants to go. I know I'm being selfish, but I get so
tired. If only Julie or Laura lived closer. Maybe I wouldn't get
so angry at being the one to carry the load.

It's not that I don't love my mother. It's just that I sometimes feel torn into so many little pieces. I have to be a faithful
daughter, a loving wife (to say nothing of being sexy and
willing at times), a good mother (who runs a taxi service on
the side), a conscientious nurse, and then with what's left, be
kind to me. I don't seem to have any time left just to be me.

Which reminds me. One of these days, I need to call Dr.

Philips and set up an appointment for a physical—the whole works, I guess. My periods have been rather irregular lately. Some of that could be due to stress, but I better have it checked out anyway.

January 12

Things are settling into a routine again after the Christmas holidays. With Matt and Megan both involved in basketball, we go to a lot of games. Or maybe I should say I do. Although once in a while, if she's feeling okay, I'll pick up Mom and take her to the game with me. She always seems to enjoy herself at the games, but it's hard to get her moving.

Gordon never seems to be home for the kids' activities these days. I remember when Matt played YMCA basketball in third and fourth grades. Gordon never missed a game. In fact, one year, he even assisted in coaching.

Nowadays Matt always asks if his dad is coming to his game. When I tell him no, he never says anything, but I can see the disappointment in his face. Matt's at an age when he really needs his dad, and I don't feel I'm a very good substitute.

Work today was such a burden. I wanted to be at home catching up on some of my work here. I always enjoyed the morning hours at home after Gordon went to work and the children were in school.

Those were my hours—my time to be by myself, to do what I wanted to do—cleaning or crafting or calling on shut-ins for the church. Now it seems all I have time for when I get home is cleaning and cooking and laundry—and, according to Gordon, I don't those do as well as I should.

I really didn't want to go back to work in the first place. And with Gordon's salary, I didn't think I needed to. But Gordon seemed to think I needed to get into the work force—fulfill myself or something.

Most days I do enjoy what I'm doing—private nursing at Oakview Manor, a retirement home just two miles from home. It's under the same management as Woodson Lakes, where Mom lives, so I know she's well cared for.

My hours are steady. I said I would come only if I had set hours during the week. I don't think I'd be able to do weekends, though Mrs. Merchent (my supervisor) has been after me to come in every other Saturday.

I can't complain about the pay either. My salary helps with Lisa's college expenses. It pays for her apartment this year, which she shares with three other girls. Plus it gives me extra for my own clothes or when I want to buy something on a whim or save for something big. That gives Gordon a chance to put a little more of his salary into savings.

Well, Gordon comes home tomorrow. Already Megan asked me if I thought her dad would be in a good mood when he arrives. These days there's no telling, but I just told Megan, "We'll plan on it."

Well, time to close the journal for another night.

January 15

Surprisingly, Gordon was in an agreeable mood when he came home a couple of days ago. Things must have gone well on his trip. He really doesn't say much about his trips anymore.

It used to be when he came home, he could sit and talk for hours. He'd always have something funny to share at the supper table, but he doesn't seem to do that much either anymore. Maybe it's because I've gotten into the habit of letting the kids eat in front of the TV when he's out of town. When Gordon comes back, it's hard to think about setting the table and sitting down to eat. Then, too, the kids' schedules are so unpredictable. It's even hard to know how many to set the table for.

I feel like I'm rambling again. Gordon's good mood lasted into this evening. Then, all of a sudden, he couldn't find any clean socks in his drawer when he was ready to play racquetball with John. The socks were clean. I just hadn't had time to bring them up from the laundry. (Mom had called just as I walked in the door after work and asked me to run her to the grocery for "a few things" again, which took an hour and a half.) When I gave Gordon his socks, he grabbed them from me, stuffed them in his bag, and stomped out of the house without saying another word.

He doesn't seem to realize that I have all the work to keep up with here at home when I get home from work. It's as bad as having two full-time jobs—sometimes three, on days I'm doing things for Mom. And some days I am so tired, I'd like to just sit and collapse. But that doesn't happen. I wonder if it's worth it.

January 21

Church and Bible class this morning. For once, Gordon came with me instead of slipping out the back door. And it's getting harder and harder to keep Matt going to the youth Bible class. He claims it's boring, that he doesn't get anything out of it. Sometimes I wonder if it wouldn't be easier to let him quit. He and Megan do go to youth-group functions quite regularly. I think we've taught our children to be independent, to think things through on their own, to make their own decisions about things. But church and Bible class are still high on my list of important things not to give them a choice about.

I wish Gordon were around more so he could talk things like this over with Matt. But because he doesn't go too often himself, I'm not sure he would encourage Matt to continue to go.

In Bible class, we're studying Philippians—the book of joy. I get so much out of the class, but somehow the joy that Paul talks about in that letter eludes me. And Gordon doesn't seem to have much of that joy these days either. I pray about it, but lately my prayers don't seem to go past the ceiling.

Mom was here for the afternoon. She helped empty some of my mending basket. We picked her up after church and took her home right after supper. There are times when I really wish Mom had learned to drive, but in this day and age, I'm glad not to worry about her going out by herself, especially in the evenings.

I'm thankful Mrs. Perkins is always so willing to pick her up to take her to over to Trinity for worship services and Bible class on Sunday mornings. She and Dad were charter members of that church. I grew up there, and I know Mom still has a few good friends there. But I know that Mom hears once a month or so of someone else who has died.

I guess it's only fair that I pick Mrs. Perkins up, too, on the nights I take Mom to her guild meeting. Mrs. Perkins does not like to drive at night—if only she didn't live in the opposite direction of Woodson Lakes, where Mom lives.

January 26

Tonight right after work, I went to Megan's basketball game. I had called Mom to see if she wanted to go, but since Matt had a game too, she thought she'd get too tired sitting through both. (Do I dare say I was secretly relieved not to make an extra trip tonight? Oh, how selfish that sounds!)

Megan's team lost by only two points—what a heart-breaker. Megan played most of the third quarter, but since there are a number of sophomores on the junior varsity team, she sat on the bench the rest of the time.

We ate at McD's (Gordon is out of town again) and then went back to the high school for Matt's game. Matt played well—made 18 points for his team, and they won. Matt enjoys basketball, and he's good at it.

I'm hoping he's offered a scholarship next year when he starts thinking about college. It sure would help out with expenses. That's another thing to put on my prayer list— helping Matt decide which college he'd like to attend. It would help a little if he knew what he wanted to do with his life, but he's very undecided at this point.

It seemed so easy when I was young. I knew from the time I was nine years old that I wanted to be a nurse. And I don't think Gordon had any trouble making business management his career. He's done well in that, though lately I'm not sure what his feelings are about his work.

Lisa, too, has wanted to teach ever since she was small. Matt and Megan don't talk about what they want to do someday. Or maybe it's that I haven't taken the time to listen.

February 1

I had been feeling so down lately. Then along comes a day like today. I went to work this morning at my usual time. I began my rounds, wondering where Dr. Jessup was. He always comes on Tuesdays and Thursdays (plus emergencies), sits in his little office, and sees residents who have unusual complaints.

When I was in with old Mr. Forebush, making him comfortable enough to have his breakfast tray brought in, I sensed another person in the room. I turned, and there he was. Not Dr. Jessup, who would have been unexpected anyway in a patient's room, but a doctor I didn't know.

Tall, with blond graying hair, gentle brown eyes, and a warm smile, he introduced himself to me. Tom Randall. Dr. Randall is taking over the next month or so for Dr. Jessup, who broke his ankle last night.

What was it about him that made me wonder where he had been all my life (boy, if that doesn't sound trite!). Tom— that's what he asked to be called—felt that to call on all patients this first time was important. He realized some of these old people are like children. They need to know of any changes taking place before they happen—or soon thereafter. He didn't want them to be frightened coming into Dr. Jessup's office and seeing a stranger sitting there.

Tom came and sat with the few of us who usually eat lunch together. It seemed to me that the whole table brightened up for the 10 minutes or so that he was there. Hmmmm. I wonder why I was able to resist the lemon meringue pie today. (The food service at the retirement home is excellent. Of course, patients and help both pay for it. Me, in more ways than one!)

Tom has been on my mind for the rest of the day. Not good! I feel on such shaky ground with Gordon these days anyway, I don't need someone like Tom Randall around to make things worse. O Lord, save me from my own thoughts!

February 6

Tom was at work again today. It's silly, but I felt like a teenager when he greeted me and told me how good it was to see me again. I feel a bit ridiculous romanticizing about him, but I get so little consideration from Gordon these days. Anyone who shows any kind of interest or kindness to me—well, I fall apart. Tom seemed to be really concerned about how I was feeling and recommended some different medication for my sinuses, which have been acting up again.

Funny, all I had to eat for lunch today was a bowl of soup and a salad. Maybe I ought to start an aerobics program at the Y. I'll have to call Colleen and ask her about it. She's been taking aerobics for several months and is looking good.

After all, Gordon's been hinting, even outright suggesting lately, that I need to shed a few pounds. I really don't need his reminders. I can see it for myself every time I look in the mirror or step on the scales! And every time he mentions it, I seem to order pie or cake for lunch just to spite him. And then I'm the one who suffers!

February 12

Gordon will be out of town until Thursday. I feel guilty, but lately, all I feel about him is relief when he's gone for a few days. And when he's due back, my stomach churns, because I wonder what he'll criticize next. I almost hold my breath waiting for it whenever he walks in the door after being gone awhile.

Other than his constant picking away at me, we don't talk or share much at all anymore. How can I defend myself against all the charges I constantly hear? I die a little inside each time. I want to, long to be closer to him. I mourn, I cry, I pray, but

134

we never seem to break any barriers. I wish I knew how to get close to him again.

We got a letter from Lisa today. She is having problems lately with Tim, the boy she's been going with quite steadily for almost two years. I'm not sure how to answer her, since I live in the midst of turmoil myself. All I can do for her, I guess, is to tell her I'm praying for her, to hang in there, and to pray about it herself. It's always easier talking these things over with her than writing. Maybe tomorrow I'll phone her.

No ball practices, no meetings, no appointments today, so I picked Mom up to bring her home to eat supper with Matt and Megan and me. Mom enjoyed herself so much. I feel so guilty that I don't do this more often, instead of making her call all the time to ask me to take her anywhere.

For some reason, it seems easier to do things for her when Gordon is out of town. Mom has a hair appointment on Wednesday that I offered to take her to, even though I'm supposed to pick up Megan from basketball practice about the same time. Well, I'll have to work something out with one of the other mothers.

February 17

I usually welcome Saturdays, for I can get caught up on some of my work. Today I did the laundry, went grocery shopping, took Mom to the Knit Shop (she's working on an afghan for sister Laura), and tonight attended the first—and last—of Matt's playoff games.

Gordon, surprisingly, went with me. Maybe he's been feeling guilty about missing all the other games. Well, the Tempests lost their game, so it puts them out of the playoffs. Matt was quite disappointed. I hurt for him, but at the same time, I'm relieved basketball is over for another season.

Matt felt for the seniors who were playing their last game. This sensitive side of Matt always catches me by surprise, yet, I guess, it really shouldn't. While he's sensitive himself to a lot of criticism, he has always seemed to hurt for others being hurt by unthinking, unfeeling people.

I feel like I got so much done today, but, of course, Gordon asked tonight if he would have any clean shirts tomorrow morning for church. Of course, there were none, and, of course, guess who got to set up the ironing board and iron a shirt at 11 o'clock at night! Why is it that I just can't keep on top of things for him? And that he always catches me at neglecting what he needs?

Oh, yes, I did call Lisa the other night. By that time she and Tim had patched up things between them. In a way, I'm glad Matt hasn't started serious dating yet. He has different girls he asks out for things coming up at school, but so far, nothing serious.

February 25

If it's not one child with a problem, it's another, or it's all three. Matt, after an almost embarrassing episode in church, finally stormed into his youth Bible class this morning. I'm sure he can't get much of anything out of the class with his attitude, but if I back down on this issue, I feel the next time I'll be fighting about whether or not he should go to church.

Megan started the day off, however, with a catastrophe in front of the mirror. Poor child, she had a zit right above one eyebrow. How could she go to church like that? I gave her some foundation powder to cover it up, but then her hair wouldn't go the right way, she complained. How come she turned out to be the ugly one of the family, she asked.

How nice it would be if children could jump from age 12 or 13 to 18 or 19 right away. Megan might not see her beauty right now, but I bet she beats even Lisa in a few years.

Megan's hair is brown with reddish highlights—she would like it to be dark like Lisa's and curly like Matt's, though she does have a perm. Her brown eyes and the few freckles across her nose just add to her impish beauty, but you can't tell a 14-year-old that.

By the time we were coming home from church, Matt wasn't speaking, but Megan was her usual cheerful self, having made plans to go to the mall with Katie, her best friend.

Gordon almost squashed that, asking why they had to make their plans so late, then who was going to drive them there and back, then why couldn't Megan stay home once in a while on a Sunday. (With that kind of atmosphere, I'm sometimes tempted to go off myself.)

When Megan called later and asked to stay at Katie's for supper, I said okay, but then had to hear the riot act again from Gordon. He doesn't seem to realize it's his own attitude the kids are avoiding when they go to their friends' homes.

March 1

Tom was at work again today. When he's there, things seem to go so much smoother. I will say that he's a great improvement over Dr. Jessup, whose ankle, by the way, isn't healing as it should. He's been ordered to stay off it for a few weeks longer.

I sure don't mind! (That doesn't sound right. I don't mean that I don't want his ankle to heal—I am sorry about that, but it does give me a chance to get to know Tom a little better.)

I talked to Tom during my break, then also during my lunch hour. He's so easy to talk to. He really seems interested in what I have to say. And he's interesting to listen to as well. That man has traveled all over the United States and Canada, and he has a story to tell about every place he has stopped.

Why is it when I'm around him, I feel needed; I feel his care and concern. In a crazy kind of way, I feel like a person— like a woman with needs and desires that aren't unimportant. I wonder if he's the reason I signed up for the aerobics class at the Y.

I have also made an appointment with my hairdresser. Gordon keeps telling me that I need to do "something different" with my hair, but before I met Tom, I never had any great desire to do it.

Oh, Lord, I need to stop feeling this way about that man. Please help me, Lord. Deliver me from myself.

March 6

Well, the gray is gone from my hair, it's styled differently, and, believe it or not, I like it! And I have lost a total of four pounds in the last week. Did I imagine it, or did Tom's eyes light up just a mite when he saw me this morning? I know that Gordon hasn't noticed at all, or, if he has, he sure hasn't said anything! I do feel better about myself. If I could lose another 8 to 10 pounds, I would really feel good! I wish taking it off were just as painless as putting it on..

Megan and even Matt said they liked my hair when I got home on Saturday after having it done. When I picked up Mom for a trip to the grocery store last night, she said it made me look younger. I told her that ought to make her feel younger, too. She just laughed.

Then I told her that she always looks good, which she does. I was surprised at how her face lit up. When I think of what compliments do for me, I am making a mental note to give my own mother more.

March 21

Today I had lunch with Colleen Denison. She asked how my "journaling" was going. I had to admit that it's been some time since I've had a chance to write. But when I do, it helps me sort out my emotions.

Before I began tonight, I looked over past entries. And I feel again that I am in the midst of chaos—mostly in my own mind. I feel that Gordon and I have reached an impasse, and I wonder if things will ever be right again.

These are the times I turn again and again to Scripture. The psalms always have something to say to me. And I cling to God's promise in Romans 8:28 that "all things God works for the good of those who love him, who have been called according to his purpose."

I do keep wondering what good will come out of this. I also remember that God will not let me be tempted above that which I am able to stand, but also will provide a way out of the temptation.

Gordon and I seem to be drifting farther and farther apart. I feel that anything I say or do—or how I look—doesn't meet his approval. He goes around the house with a constant frown on his face.

I wonder if my unhappiness shows as much as his does. But nothing I do for him or say to him makes any difference. He's still super critical, still finds fault with everything. Matt and Megan notice his attitude too and stay out of his way.

Lisa brought Tim home last weekend, and Gordon tensed up even more. He did seem to relax a little more after they were gone, but it didn't last past Monday morning. Lisa asked me a couple of times what was wrong with her dad, but how could I tell her when I don't even know myself?

I find more things to talk to Dr. Tom Randall about at work—though never about what is eating away at me. Tom always makes me feel good about myself, then I go home and *wham!* I get hit with a bunch of negatives again. Sometimes I'm tempted to walk out and leave it all behind. If it weren't for the kids ... What would they say? What would they do? Dear Lord, hang on to me!

March 26

Gordon left for another out-of-town trip today. He'll be gone until Thursday. I always feel relieved for awhile when he's gone, but I then feel guilty for being able to "be myself" for a few days.

Megan right now is struggling with a friend at school. She and Katie have always been close, but since Megan has been playing basketball, she is getting to know some of the other freshmen girls a little better. Since Katie doesn't play, she often feels left out and thinks Megan doesn't like her as well as she does the other girls.

I keep thinking how simple life was when the children were smaller. I wish I could put a Band-Aid on a relationship as easily as I put one on skinned knees, that a little glue and tape would fix feelings as easily as they did broken toys. I wish I could stop this world from spinning too fast as quickly as I washed dirty hands in days that disappeared before I was ready for them to.

Listening seems to be the key for both Matt and Meg these days. And to me that's more important than ironing shirts or balancing the checkbook (though I can't tell Gordon that).

I've gotten a lot of compliments on my hair. I'm glad I got it styled at the same time I got the gray covered. People notice the different style, not that the gray is gone. Also, I have lost another three pounds since I "journaled" the last time.

March 28

I have been sitting in my bedroom, staring into space for the past hour and a half. I finally had an appointment today with my gynecologist. The problems I've had with my periods have not gone away.

I used to be able to tell by the calendar when I'd get my next one, but for the past several months they have been unpredictable. Some have been rather skimpy, too. When this last one was two weeks late, I thought I'd better have it checked.

After the examination, Dr. Philips asked me a few questions. Then she told me I was probably at the start of menopause. I could feel my mouth drop open. I told her, "I'm too young for that!" She asked how old I was.

I said, "Forty-five."

She shook her head gently and said, "It comes to all of us sooner or later, and yours just happens to be sooner than you expected." We talked for a good long while, then she gave me some literature to read and a prescription for hormone pills. As I left, she said, "Think of it, Abby, as a new beginning, not the end."

But I am still in shock. I'm not ready to become "an older woman," but suddenly I feel as old as my mother. The sudden knowledge that I will no longer have the capacity to bear children weighs strangely heavily upon me, even though we had made the decision after Megan not to have any more children, and we had really never planned on having another child. I guess it's just the fact that it's no longer a choice.

In a way, I'm glad Gordon won't be back until Saturday. If I can't talk to him about everyday happenings, how can I ever talk to him about what I'm going through now?

Lord, I'm so glad You are still close beside me, listening to me, knowing my grief, for in a way I feel a death has occurred. I need You, Lord, to lift me up, to pour Your own strength into me, for I have none of my own. O Lord, I need You, for I don't have anyone else.

March 31

Gordon arrived home today in a foul mood. No greeting, no kiss, just, "Where's the paper?" and "Why isn't supper on the table yet? You knew I'd be home by 6:30." He's already in bed, probably asleep with his back to the middle of the bed.

I sit here as tears stream down my face. I seem to have no control over them these days. I cry for myself, for a me I don't know anymore and for the me I used to be. I just don't know what to do. My own physical and emotional needs seem overwhelming right now. But my prayers seem to fall on deaf ears as I ask the Lord for relief.

I cry for Gordon. I know he must be hurting way deep inside. But I can't get through to him anymore. And I sometimes wonder if he has quit loving me. And even worse, I wonder if I have stopped loving him.

April 2

I took a day off work today. Colleen and I had lunch together, and we had a long talk. At least she's one person I can count on to listen to me without a lecture afterward. And I know she's gone through much of what I'm experiencing right now. She told me that it was at the onset of menopause that she began keeping a journal. She did warn me that when she was going through menopause, she really began to mistrust her own judgments, her own capacity for thinking clearly. "I made such dumb mistakes at times," she told me. "But," she added, "it does pass." I thanked her for the warning. Colleen assured me, too, just as Dr. Philips had, that it's not the end of the world (though how come I still think it is?).

April 4

I can't believe it! I just can't believe it! Gordon has gone off and purchased a speedboat that we'll be making payments on for the next 10 years! No consultation, no "let's look this over, Hon." No "what do you think?" I'm so mad I could spit nails. I protested going to work because we really didn't need the money. Gordon said it would "fulfill" me.

My salary is paying for Lisa's apartment, and I have a fair amount set aside for a rainy-day project. But a boat! It's just too much! I know Gordon has talked about getting one off and on for several years, but to go out and sign papers on it without any kind of discussion!!!!

Of course Matt is thrilled. He and Gordon are already talking about fishing trips. Even Megan is caught up in it. She would love to learn to waterski. And me—I get deathly ill walking out on a pier, much less setting foot on a boat.

Right now I'm so mad, I don't know what I'll do. Maybe book a European vacation for myself!

April 6

Now Gordon is mad at me. I just told him tonight that people were coming tomorrow to measure the living and dining rooms for drapes. We have needed them for so long. I've mentioned it to Gordon any number of times, but I don't think it ever sank in. But now, if we have money for a boat, we certainly have money for new drapes.

Maybe I will tell Gordon tomorrow that I've got money saved up for the drapes. It won't be any of his precious money that will pay for them.

I'm certainly not in a very good mood tonight. I feel resentful, guilty, angry, but, I must add, a bit triumphant, too.

April 10

My mom came for Easter last Sunday. Gordon's parents left last week for their annual trip to California to visit Dad's sister and Gordon's younger brother.

Church was packed on Easter. I sure needed the message of joy in the resurrected Christ. I know I am forgiven—saved for heaven, even if I don't always feel it. And my feelings certainly aren't forgiveness oriented these days.

When Mom saw Gordon's boat, she raised her eyebrows and looked at me, but I wouldn't talk about it. I didn't even want to think about it. Gordon was enthusiastic as he showed off the boat. I wish I could rejoice with him, but all I feel are anger and disappointment.

The only thing that keeps me going right now is knowing I'll see Dr. Tom Randall every Tuesday and Thursday and feel that someone is concerned and cares about me.

But this isn't the way things are supposed to go. I don't want to fall in love with someone else. I just want to go back to loving Gordon, to getting in a right relationship with him. But how do I do that? Which way is up?

April 12

A note of joy in this mad world of mine. Sister Julie called today. She said Dan is being transferred to the main office of his company just 25 miles from here. They will be moving this summer. Julie, God bless her, said she is anxious to help out with some running around for Mom, taking her out to their place on weekends, and such.

143

When I told Gordon, he smiled and said, "Well, that's good news now, isn't it?" It's silly, but I almost cried when he said that. I feel like those are the first kind words he has said to me in months. He and Dan have always gotten along, thank the Lord, so I know he won't mind their company now and then.

When I told Julie about Gordon's boat, she was surprised. She knows how I am about water. But we didn't have a chance to talk long. Johnny and Rachel were having a small fight in the background. Oh, it will be fun to have those two little ones so close by!

April 19

Well, I should have expected it. It's kind of the crowning blow to the last few weeks. Tom told me today that Dr. Jessup is finally returning next Tuesday and this was his last day. In much too casual a tone, he said he'd miss my friendship, but that maybe he'd come back for a visit sometime.

As much as he really did seem to enjoy my company and the work of the nursing home, I have to be honest with myself. I don't think he'll be back. It hurts to say that. I miss him so much already. I'd like to just bury my head in the sand and let the rest of the world go by for a few weeks. O Lord, hang on to me!

April 21

I'm still sputtering! Gordon announced today that he wants to go up to the lake tomorrow morning and take Matt along. Tomorrow is Sunday! I can't believe this. And with all the trouble I have getting Matt to go to church anyway!

I guess I should be thankful that he didn't want to take Megan too, though she wanted to ride along. (Thank goodness it's too cold to waterski yet.) I am going to have to muster my forces! Lord, help me know what to do, what to say.

I can't believe I've done it. I'm sitting in the guest room at my sister Laura's as I write this. The 200-mile drive to Laura's place was tiring. I have been here since late yesterday afternoon.

After church yesterday morning, Pastor Sanders asked me where Gordon and Matt were. All of a sudden, everything crashed in on me. I wanted Gordon and Matt to be there with me. I wanted our family to be whole and healthy again. I wanted to be the calm easygoing, patient, cheerful (well, most of the time) woman I remember myself being in days gone by.

I can't remember anymore what I said to Pastor Sanders. Somehow I sat through Bible class, barely making it. I just wanted to go somewhere and scream! So I came to Laura's instead.

Katie had invited Megan to spend the day with her. I went home, changed, and began straightening things up in the house. While I was putting some pens and pencils away in Gordon's desk, I got another look at the bill for the boat. That's when I decided I couldn't handle it any longer.

After throwing some things in a suitcase, I called Megan at Katie's and told her to wait for her dad's call. Then I wrote a short message to Gordon, telling him I needed to get away for awhile. I said I was going to visit Laura, that they shouldn't worry about me, and that I would let them know in a day or two when I would be home.

Next I called the nursing home and said that an emergency had called me out of town for a few days (which is a fact, though I don't know if the emergency would be mine or Gordon's).

Finally I called Laura and asked how she would like a visit from her little sister. Laura asked no questions, just said, "I'll have a room ready for you."

That's the good thing about Laura. She never pries, but once you get started, she listens well! She is the one Julie and I always turned to when we were little and needed help with anything and Mom couldn't give us her full attention at the time.

Laura has never married. While she had her share of boy-friends growing up, she never got serious about any of them. She claims she doesn't miss married life at all. These days, I'm inclined to envy her.

Laura owns her own comfortable home, and she settled me into her guest bedroom as soon as I arrived. We ate the chicken salad she had prepared for supper, washed the dishes, then sat on her little patio, talking over cups of coffee until almost midnight (we did move inside to the den when it got too cold outside). We reminisced mostly about our young years at home, our growing-up years.

This morning Laura left early for her work at the local hospital. She is the day supervisor there, only second in com-mand to the head honcho.

Tonight Laura listened well. Very casually, she asked how Gordon and the kids were. Just that simple question set off the tears. I broke down and must have cried for half an hour. Then I told her about Gordon and me, about Matt's problems in going to Bible class, about Megan's problems with Katie, of how I have a hard time letting them grow up and handle their own problems.

I told her about Dr. Tom and my feelings for him. I told her about the boat and the new drapes. I told her about my work and my fears of "growing old" and all the physical changes happening to me right now.

Laura sat quietly for a few minutes, then asked me to pray with her. My gracious! I thought I knew how to pray. But Laura gets right up there next to God's throne and talks with Him as Megan used to go to Gordon and ask him to fix her doll's broken arm or the wheels on her roller skates.

After her prayer, Laura asked me point-blank if I was think-ing about divorce. "Oh, my, no!" I told her. "As much as I'm hurting, and as much as I know Gordon is hurting, I know that I can't even think about divorce. I made a commitment in my marriage vows, and I aim to keep them. No, divorce for me is not an option."

"Good," Laura said. "That's a point in everyone's favor."

146

Then she asked me a very strange question—or so I thought at the time. She asked what acts of love I had done for Gordon lately. I've done more than he's done for me, but I didn't want to argue. I told her I didn't understand.

"Look, Abby," she said. "I may not be married, but I do know a little about caring for and caring about other people." She went on to tell me about a patient who had come into the hospital for an extended stay. Not long after he arrived, the nurses in that section were complaining up one side and down the other about this patient. He turned everyone off. He didn't like the food; his medication was not the right strength. The nurses weren't making his bed just right; his drinking water was too cold or too warm.

Because of having to juggle vacation times for the nurses, one of the nurses from pediatrics was transferred for a week to that section. Not long afterwards, different comments were coming from the nurses about that patient. What had changed him? Just simple acts of love.

He had come to the hospital, he thought, to die. That scared him, but he couldn't let anyone know about his fears. So he was cantankerous and unpleasant. Definitely not a good patient. And the regular nurses were letting him dictate their feelings. Then they acted on their feelings, not to his need.

When Nurse Edwards went in there, she always answered his complaints with a smile. She pulled the bedsheet a little tighter, said she'd check with the doctor about the strength of his medication, and ordered some special, more appetizing meals for him. When the patient realized that someone really cared enough about him to listen to him and act on his complaints, he felt cared for and loved. While he didn't change completely or overnight, he was a much more tractable patient.

Then Laura hit me with the message I think I've been looking for all along. She said that God loves us, but His love showed itself in action. He saw our need for saving and acted on it by sending Jesus to die for us.

When we know we love someone, but our feelings don't match our knowledge, we need to make our love show itself in action. The feelings are secondary. They follow the action.

Sometimes we must force ourselves to do the acts of love, but gradually the feeling of love will also come. At the time, my thought was *maybe.*

I have to remember not to rely on my feelings, because they come and go. Deep down inside I know I still love Gordon. And I must believe that he loves me. Now to do the love—to act—even if he doesn't respond.

April 25

Wow, was that last entry long. I must have sat up until two o'clock in the morning to write that all down.

I called Gordon today to let him know I would be driving home tomorrow morning. Do you know, he almost sounded happy to hear it!

I've been doing a lot of thinking and praying the last couple days. I know a lot of the things I've done for Gordon I have not done out of love, but out of guilt and self-preservation. I have an idea that it's going to be a long way back, and not easy either, but walk it I will.

Maybe I'll take time to sit with Matt and Megan more and listen to their concerns, not just force my own will on them without any other input. I need to let them know—as I did with Lisa—why things are important and why I won't back down on some issues.

I have a feeling I'm going to need lots of prayer and lots of direction from the Lord.

April 26

I can't believe it! Gordon actually hugged and kissed me when I got home today. I'm not sure if Matt and Megan really know the undercurrent of all that's been going on, but they sure looked happy and relieved to see me again.

Tonight was Gordon's and my time to talk. He opened up a little, and I opened up a little. I asked him—gently, I think—

what the real reason was he wanted me to go back to work. He hesitated but finally told me his job had been in jeopardy. At first he thought it would all blow over quickly, but that my having a job would make us more secure in any case.

When the problem lingered, he felt uncomfortable telling me. He didn't want to seem like a bad provider and put the burden of the family's welfare on my shoulders. His job became strongly secure again just before Easter—and that's when he bought the new boat.

We both cried a little, apologized a lot, laughed a little, and hugged a lot. Oh my, what anguish he has been going through this past year or so. And I haven't made it any easier for him.

Well, there's still all this business about the boat, but I hope we work through that one as well. If we do, maybe the drape issue will take care of itself.

I know I have a lot to look forward to. A closer relationship with God—and another one with Gordon, when he let's it happen. A chance to enjoy the teen years with my (whoops! our) kids—is that possible? I do miss their young years, but God helping me, I can get closer to them in other ways.

May 2

Well, a few setbacks this past week. I knew it wouldn't be easy. Right now I'm dealing with some anger at Gordon for not sharing his burden with me. Didn't he trust me? Did he think I wasn't strong enough? O Lord, help me forgive. And Lord, I know I haven't always met Gordon's needs, nor have I been open in sharing my needs with him. Forgive me for that and help me do better.

I will say that even with Dr. Tom gone, things at work are going better. Maybe it's because I don't resent so much being at work anymore.

The big news is that Lisa and Tim visited this past weekend, and she displayed the diamond he gave her. He formally asked Gordon's and my permission to marry our daughter, which we gladly gave.

They plan to finish college. They both have another year to go. But I'm not sure I'm ready for another whole set of different problems—or should I call them opportunities—that of being a mother-in-law and eventually—maybe, someday— a grandma.

An Encouraging Word

Abby's situation seems similar to many other women in mid-life who have been devoted wives and mothers. She sounds like a woman who cares deeply for her husband and her children, but she knows something has gone wrong. Someone has let the air out of her balloon. Her dream of what life would be like when her family was grown is not coming true. This is no longer the ideal, perfect family. On the surface to outsiders it all looks well, but Abby, using her sixth sense, knows something is not right. Something is very wrong.

Abby faces a new problem, one she has never before had to face. Something is wrong with her husband. There is definitely a change in his behavior, a change in his attitude. Something has happened to his self-esteem. He is no longer able to fulfill expectations for himself as a good husband and father. He undoubtedly equates his self-worth with his ability to be a good provider.

As the male in the family, Gordon feels he should be strong and carry this burden alone. He feels very angry at himself for not having a secure job, and he is having difficulty facing the fact that he may not be able to provide for his wife and children. Afraid and ashamed, he begins dumping his feelings, his criticism of himself, onto Abby.

Abby is completely unaware of the internal struggle Gordon is facing. He faces it alone. He handles it himself.

For a while Abby receives all of his self-loathing, all of his anger toward himself. She becomes the receptacle, the garbage can for his negative feelings. The weight of his depression and anger is heavy. His depression and anger slowly are transferred to Abby. Unfortunately, she also decides to carry the weight of this burden alone.

A negative, self-destructive cycle has developed. Gordon is depressed and feeling angry at himself. He tries to hide it. Instead it comes out in criticism of Abby. Abby accepts the undeserved criticism and becomes depressed herself. She, too, decides to hide her feelings of low self-worth and begins feeling unloved, rejected, and angry at Gordon. She blames him for her distress and becomes stuck in a critical, negative way of thinking and behaving.

There is a missing piece or link. Unfortunately, neither Abby nor Gordon can find this missing link that would end the deterioration in their marriage.

The boat is Gordon's attempt to lift this dark veil that has fallen over his life and the life of his family. The boat is a good idea, but not effective, especially for Abby.

The drapes are Abby's attempt to feel some relief from this inescapable pain. For a moment she feels triumphant.

However, this short-lived joy backfires, further damaging the relationship and leaving her with guilt. Purchasing the drapes ends up making the problem worse. Abby feels worse. The black hole of depression, despair, rejection, and pain continues to deepen.

Relief seems impossible. It seems that Abby's and Gordon's marriage is over. Their psychological, spiritual, and, one would assume, sexual bonding had ended. The only thing they seem capable of doing together is dumping their negative feelings on each other and blaming each other for their individual misery.

Abby is finally able to break the cycle of false bravado and holding in her feelings. Finally the negative cycle begins to crack.

The move towards peace, health, life, and reconciliation began for Abby while she was at church. Many women are able to deny and repress their feelings during a busy week at work and home. Very often feelings begin surfacing at church with time to sit, to relax, to feel God's presence. Many women use this time for self-reflection and for getting in touch with their feelings and their current situation. When someone like

Abby's pastor asks about her family, her buried feelings begin to surface. They are much too strong and come much too quickly for Abby to be able to deal with them comfortably alone. Her defenses are down. The pain has surfaced. She knows she needs to do something different to break the cycle, to relieve the pain. She phones her sister and travels to see her. Getting away from the situation gives Abby a chance to evaluate objectively what is happening to her.

Having a caring friend (a sister) she could trust was a blessing to Abby. No longer did she have to carry this burden alone. All of the pain, the hurt, the frustration, the feeling of rejection she had been journaling came pouring out. Another human being was there to listen.

What a friend Laura turned out to be! She was kind and supportive. She accepted Abby and her feelings. She listened. At the same time Laura began to give a new perspective to the situation. Laura was beginning to see a possible missing link—love and concern for the other. She helped Abby get in touch with her own passivity about the situation. Laura opened Abby's eyes to new thoughts, new ideas. She spoke of God's love, God's acts of love. She put Abby in touch with the possibility of doing something besides feeling sorry for herself.

When Abby heard the new but forgotten idea of showing love to her husband, it was as if a dim light was beginning to illuminate the dark hole she had been living in the past several months. That dim light grew stronger as she began thinking about implementing her new plan.

The missing link had been found—acts of love, assertiveness. A series of these acts of love had touched and influenced Abby herself in those significant few days when her life was turning around. First there was the quiet time in church surrounded by God's love. Then there was the pastor reaching out to Abby and her family with love and concern. This seemed to help give Abby the strength, the potency to reach out to another woman. She went to Laura. Laura cared, which allowed Abby to talk about her feelings.

Abby became energized to reach out to her husband with a new attitude, with a positive caring touch. Her openness and ability to be vocal and assertively caring allowed Gordon to reciprocate. First he revealed the secret burden he had been carrying for so long, and then he reached out again to his dear but psychologically shriveling wife with the touch of love and concern.

The openness, caring, and respect these two almost estranged people began showing toward one another broke the negative cycle for both of them. There was no going back. They again appreciated the positive strokes they were receiving from one another.

Perhaps, they each silently renewed their marriage vows, recommitting themselves to one another under God. Perhaps, the caring and touching were there the evening she returned home, the next morning, the next day, and the next week. The cycle had definitely been reversed. Abby and Gordon could touch again emotionally, physically, and spiritually. The power and love of God was again alive and well in their marriage.

What about Tom? What part did he temporarily play in Abby's life? He was a reminder to her that her life could be different, that her relationships could be different. Relationships could be more positive. Abby appreciated the reminder. Tom was kind. Abby was attracted to his warmth. It was a secret, emotional reaching out, a schoolgirl crush, a tempting, brief fantasy, comic relief in the midst of a painful marriage relationship. If Tom had been seeking a new intimate relationship, he might have found Abby vulnerable. Abby's story could have had a different ending, and the confusion in her life might have increased.

Likewise, the children and their activities provided temporary relief. However, there was not enough positive reinforcement coming from the children. They had their own lives now. They didn't need Abby in the same way as they had in the past. Moreover, it is not the role of children to make up for marital unhappiness within the family. Making the children responsible for Abby's emotional needs could have hindered their own personal development.

Abby needed someone to care about her plight. She needed to experience God's acceptance and gentleness through another human being. That happened through her pastor, through Laura, and ultimately through Gordon.

Abby is a wise woman. As she closes this segment of her journal, she realizes that are many obstacles in a person's life. Gordon and she will face many roadblocks and trials as the years pass by. Many traps lie along the way to draw them back into the negative cycle of being closed emotionally, physically, and spiritually.

Hopefully, they both have learned how to assertively restore the relationship.

Hopefully, they have been reminded again of what they can do to live life to the fullest in a positive relationship.

A Note to Women in Midlife

Abby was blessed with a pastor, a sister, and a husband who could reciprocate. The give-and-take of love worked well in her life. She had people who could catch the ball of love and pass it on or toss it back to her. She had people in her life who were willing to play with her in this game of life with a helpful, winning attitude.

It is not so easy for many women in middle age. Sometimes it is necessary to develop *new* relationships and to add *new* friends in order to maintain adequate avenues of support.

Most women experience a multitude of changes in midlife. Some women have not thought about their lives beyond the day when their children will leave home. Much of their identity has been tied up in the little word *mom.* With the end of the mothering role, a woman often simultaneously experiences changes in her body, the end of her menstrual cycle and her childbearing years. Her external beauty begins to pale with sagging here and there and with the appearance of tiny laugh lines around the eyes or new wrinkles in the cheeks. These are signs of a new stage.

Many husbands begin to notice a deterioration in their own health and bodies. On the job they begin to experience threats of being replaced with younger, cheaper, less-experienced workers.

Middle age is not an easy time for husbands or wives, and yet it can be viewed as the beginning of a new adventure, the beginning of a new phase of life. It's different from the twenties and thirties, which had other distinct problems and challenges. Most women will live to be 75 or 80 or older. Most women will spend 5 to 15 years without a mate. Midlife is a good time for a woman to take stock of who she is. It is a good time for her to ask what purpose God might have for her in the last half of her life.

It's time for her to begin to look at what kind of shape she is in physically. It's time for her to think of adding a physical fitness program to her busy schedule. It's time for her to walk a few miles a day or to do low-impact aerobics in front of the VCR.

It's time for a woman to reexamine her diet. Her metabolism usually begins to slow down as physical activity decreases. Perhaps she is beginning to add unwanted and unneeded pounds. It's time for a physical examination by an M.D. It's time to cut back on sugar, caffeine, fat, and cholesterol.

A good way for a woman to reassess who she is emotionally and spiritually is to begin journaling like Abby. Writing down her thoughts and feelings on a consistent basis and then reading the journal after some time has passed can help a woman to see herself from a different perspective. Journaling might point a woman in a new direction. Like Abby she might also realize she is trying to carry some burden alone. The journaling might reveal a dream yet unfulfilled. Journaling is one way for a woman to begin taking stock of where she is emotionally and spiritually.

Often a woman postpones her personal goals in life, because she wants to help her husband establish his career and because she wants to care for her children and give them every advantage. In midlife things are different. Her husband is established vocationally, and her children are almost gone. Midlife is a time to establish new goals. It's not too late to think of starting a new career or developing an old one.

As the years pass by there may be more time for reading Scripture, for meditating, for spending time with God.

Hobbies should not be forgotten. Reading, gardening, sports, cooking, and traveling can bring a ray of delight and satisfaction to life. For the woman who enjoys these or other activities, a new dimension could be added to her life.

Midlife is an exciting and adventuresome time of life for the assertive woman. She has much knowledge about herself and others. She usually has some resources in friends, talents, or treasures. She still has a lot of energy, and she has learned to do many things quickly and efficiently.

Her husband need not be left out of a new adventure. He too might enjoy a new experience.

Abby became overwhelmed with the lack of communication along with the midlife changes and became depressed. Signs of depression include feeling blue, hopeless, and rejected; experiencing a lack of energy; crying; changes in sleep patterns and appetite.

If the adjustment to midlife changes seems too overwhelming, and if talking to friends or family does not help, a woman should not hesitate to seek professional help. Her pastor, deaconess, family doctor, counselor, or psychiatrist will be able to give her a more objective, supportive view of her situation and herself. In some cases, medication might be helpful to aid her through the hormonal changes or to combat a complicated depression.

A woman in pain, caught in a negative cycle of depression, does not need to carry the burden alone. God has blessed her with many caring people, who, in the name of Jesus, are there for her.

For that woman and for all women in midlife, it is a time to reach out, to be assertive in grappling with change, and to set new goals for the adventure that is yet to be.

Shirley Schaper

Reflection

- Which of Abby's problems remind you of your own problems?

- With whom do you feel comfortable sharing your experiences and your feelings?

- God answers your prayers. He uses other people to draw you closer to Him. He shows you the direction He wants you to go. Whom is God using in your life right now? Who listens to you without making you feel guilty? How long since you talked—and prayed—with that person?

- In the epistles, the words *one another* appear almost 60 times. Christians are urged to care for one another ... encourage one another ... edify ... teach ... comfort and support one another. Who needs you most right now? Friend? Children? Parent? Spouse?

- Read the encouraging word in 1 Corinthians 10:13. List times when God has led you out of difficulty and confusion to victory and understanding. Thank Him for those times.

- Set some personal goals for yourself. Do it today. Spend time with God in his Word for direction in your goal setting.

- Remember, God loves you. God is faithful. He is the promise-keeper. He will keep you safe from the tricks of the devil, strengthen your love for others, and give you courage and joy in Him every day—in every season—of your life.

Dear Lord,

Today I don't feel quite myself,
I cry and feel so dumb, Lord.
But I take comfort in Your Word
And know *You* never change.

The burdens seem so different now
From when I was much younger.
I had more joy, more energy,
I was, oh, so much stronger.

I thought that with the vow I spoke
There's nothing we couldn't conquer;
Together we faced each day alike,
And how we loved each other.

But things have changed so drastically,
I'm not sure where I'm going.
But I find comfort, knowing this,
You're with me as I'm growing.

And as I change, please be with me.
Forgive when I go wrong, Lord.
And keep me serving You each day,
For this is what I long for.

And so I pray for strength and joy,
For health, and peace, and reason.
I pray for sanity (not wealth)
To reach all those who need me.

And when demands are great or small,
Let me rely on You, Lord.
Your strength will fill my weaknesses;
Your love will be my joy.

And Lord, please let there be each day,
If only just a minute,
That I can take time for myself
And know that You are in it.

Amen.